TSUNAMI

A Novel

Published by TriMark Press, Inc., Deerfield Beach, Florida.

Library of Congress Cataloging-in-Publication Data

Tsunami
Watson, Alessandro and Robert P. Watson

p. cm.

ISBN: 978-0-9849568-3-8
Library of Congress Control Number: 2012947981

H12
10 9 8 7 6 5 4 3 2 1
First Edition, Fiction
Printed and Bound in the United States of America

publishing the written word
trimarkpress

A publication of TriMark Press, Inc.
368 South Military Trail
Deerfield Beach, FL 33442
800.889.0693
www.TriMarkPress.com

TSUNAMI

A Novel

Alex Watson & Robert P. Watson

PUBLISHED BY TRIMARK PRESS, INC.
800.889.0693
WWW.TRIMARKPRESS.COM

Acknowledgments

When Alex proposed to Robert the idea of writing a book together it was one of those "eureka" moments for us. For the past few years, teachers, psychologists, and politicians have been encouraging parents and their children to read together. But, why not write a book together? As fun and meaningful as it is to read together, it is an altogether more rewarding experience to write together.

So, we hope not only that you enjoy this adventure story, but that it inspires you to write a book with a friend or family member. In fact, we created a website dedicated to helping parents and children write books together – www.LetsWriteTogether.com.

There are a few individuals who helped us with the book and we would like to acknowledge them. It has been a delight to work with the talented and supportive team at

TriMark Press. So, to Barry Chesler, Penelope Love, and Hina Shaikh, we offer our sincere appreciation for your interest in this book. Thanks also to Ashley Ford, who offered several good ideas for our "Let's Write Together" website.

Thank you to Grandmother Celeste who helped to inspire the book. Of course, we also thank Claudia and Isabella for their patience during the time it took us to write the book.

Alex Watson and Robert Watson
Boca Raton, Florida

Glossary of Hawaiian Terms

A'a – Sharp, stony lava

Aina – The land

Malama Aina – Love and caring for the land

Ali'i – A chief or king; Hawaiian royalty

Aloha – A greeting such as hello; love

Da Kine – A slang word that means anything you want; used in place of "thing"

E komo mai – Welcome

Halema'uma'u – A large, active crater on the side of Mauna Loa and Kilauea volcanoes

Hula – A dance or song

Imu – An underground oven used to cook pig

Kapu – Taboo or forbidden

Ka'u – The southernmost point of the Big Island of Hawaii

Kilauea – The world's most active volcano, located on the side of Mauna Loa, the world's largest volcano

King Kamehameha – The first king of the Hawaiian islands

Lei – A necklace of flowers, leaves, or shells

Luau – A Hawaiian feast

Madam Pele – The goddess who lives in the volcano

Mahalo – Thank you

Malamalama – From "malama," which means to take care of or serve, as in God; a sacred woman

Malihini – A newcomer to Hawaii or a guest

Mauka – In the direction of the mountains

Ono – Delicious or tasty

Plumeria – An ornamental and popular flower in Hawaii, often used to make leis

Pua'a – Pig or boar

Puka – To make a hole through something; a small, shell necklace

Pu'u O'o – An active lava vent on Kilauea Volcano

Shaka – A popular Hawaiian hand gesture used for friendship or as a greeting

Ti – A popular long-leafed plant in Hawaii that comes in reds and greens

Tiki hut – A hut that is thatched with palms

Chapter 1

Vacation

"What could possibly go wrong?" John Sanders said wryly to his wife, his raised eyebrows giving away his true feelings. Mr. Sanders could not contain his emotions any longer. Shaking his head, he continued: "I mean, gee, the kid's nickname is Spike. What is wrong with that picture?"

"I know," his wife Clara replied. She exhaled slowly and calmly, but deeply. They had been through this discussion before.

Clara and John had planned what they thought would be their family's perfect "vacation of a lifetime." But the ten-day trip to Hawaii in June after the school year ended had run into two surprising obstacles. One was their son, Isaac, and the other was their daughter, Rebecca.

Isaac was finishing middle school at the North Lake School

and his sister was a few years behind him, proud that she had just completed her last year at the town's lower school.

It was easy to tell that the two were siblings. They both had large, blue eyes and shared the same facial features, including the trademark Sanders family smile. It was a warm smile, one that radiated as much from the eyes as from the lips. The resemblance between brother and sister was something the teachers at school frequently mentioned to Rebecca. Without exception, the start of classes every new school year was the same for her: "Oh, you must be the sister of Isaac Sanders!" But that was not the worst part of it.

Such comments were usually followed by the teacher saying, "Isaac was one of my best students. What a lucky girl you are to have such a smart brother!" Rebecca always smiled back, but in truth, she felt like rolling her eyes. She and her brother were close – naturally, they had the usual brother-sister arguments – but she grew tired of the constant comparisons.

There were differences between them, however. Rebecca had long, dark hair that was usually tied back in a neat, tight bow; Isaac had notoriously unruly hair. A wave of dirty blond hair always curled outward from beside his left ear, giving him a perpetual windblown look. Even when Mrs. Sanders combed his hair or added some of the gel he hated, the hair would eventually win the battle. After a few minutes – pop! A large curl swooped like the Nike shoe logo out from beside Isaac's ear. For the most part, Isaac and Rebecca were friendly, despite the incident that happened five years earlier.

Rebecca was also a bit nervous about starting middle school the next year. Isaac's teasing didn't help things. He knew about Rebecca's natural apprehensiveness. But, like all good brothers, it was his duty to tease his sister.

"Leave your sister alone," was Mrs. Sanders' usual reply to her son. "Don't listen to him, Rebecca, middle school is just like lower school. Only more fun!"

After trying to reassure her daughter, Mrs. Sanders always gave Isaac one of those looks that only a mother could give, telling him without words to stop worrying his sister... or else!

Perhaps Isaac's teasing was the reason Rebecca did not want to go to Hawaii. Or at least that is what their parents thought. Both John and Clara Sanders were shocked to find that their children were not excited about the big family vacation when they informed them. Much to Isaac's embarrassment, his parents had even purchased plastic flower leis – the cheap kind sold at the local party supply store each summer – to go along with the surprise vacation announcement. But the grand surprise went over like a lead balloon.

When Isaac and Rebecca walked through the front door after the last day of the school year, they were greeted with a scream of "Aloha!" Both parents stood in the living room wearing the leis over brightly colored Hawaiian shirts. Hawaiian music played in the living room.

Some surprise. Mr. and Mrs. Sanders expected their children to be thrilled with the prospects of a trip to the exotic Pacific islands. Isaac, after all, had a poster of a surfer in Hawaii's famous pipeline on the wall of his bedroom. But neither child was enthusiastic. Both parents had noticed that their children were now at that age where they seemed less and less interested in traveling anywhere with their family. Also, over the past few weeks, the parents noticed that their children seemed to have less to say to them. Each day when they asked Isaac and Rebecca how their school day had gone, for example, the reply had gone from a monotone "Yea, good" to a dull expression and shrug of the shoulders. Mr. and Mrs. Sanders therefore hoped that the Hawaiian vacation would rekindle those fun, family times.

Clara Sanders had begun to describe the fancy hotel where they would be staying but Isaac walked past his parents to his room, followed by Rebecca who headed for her room. John and Clara Sanders just looked blankly at one another.

So that was why Mr. and Mrs. Sanders reluctantly agreed to allow both children to invite one of their friends from school to join the family on the vacation – with friends along, the Sanders' children were more likely to be excited about the trip. Isaac had overheard his mother explaining to his father, "The kids want to be with their friends. What's wrong with bringing along two extra children?" Isaac's father was hardly convinced. John Sanders was not thrilled with the idea but the big vacation might be saved and if anyone could talk him into such an arrangement, it was Mrs. Sanders.

Petite but full of life, Mrs. Sanders bubbled over with enthusiasm about most everything. When she talked, she did so with her hands waving and a restlessness that revealed her excitement. And so it was as she presented the case to her husband to allow the kids to pick one friend each to travel with them to Hawaii.

Rebecca's best friend, Grace, was not a problem. Grace's family lived three houses down the street and both families were very close, with Grace spending as much time at the Sanders' home as Rebecca spent at Grace's home. The girls were even in the same class at school and both shared a polite and chatty disposition. Plus, Grace had been a constant help after Rebecca's accident a few years ago. After only a few minutes, the sale worked and John Sanders was on board with the decision.

But Mr. Sanders assumed that his son would invite Kevin O'Connell. Kevin was one of Isaac's closest friends and the two were in the Hiking Club together at school and played in a youth baseball league that year. The Sanders and O'Connell families knew each other well. Kevin he could handle.

But to Mr. Sanders' dismay, Isaac added his own surprise announcement. He informed his family that he wanted to invite the new kid in his class, Spike.

"What is his real name?" asked Mr. Sanders with a disapproving scowl visible on his face.

"Leonard," responded Isaac.

"No wonder he has a nickname," smirked Isaac's father.

"Now John!" Isaac's mother looked sternly at her husband. "I am sure Leonard – or, ah Spike – is a good kid." But Mrs. Sanders looked unconvinced. She nervously started playing with her hair, rolling small strands of it with her index finger, a sure sign that she was concerned. She always did this when she was worried.

"Are you sure you want to invite him, Isaac?" his mother asked. "We hardly know his parents."

Mrs. Sanders had only briefly met Spike's mother twice when she pulled up at their house looking for her son. Spike lived in the neighborhood next to where the Sanders lived, and he occasionally played with Isaac, riding his skateboard loudly up the cobblestone walkway of the Sanders' home. Spike's neighborhood was what Mrs. Sanders politely called "unfortunate." Isaac had correctly guessed what that meant.

"Sure, mom," Isaac answered. He seemed a little less resistant to the Hawaiian vacation as he spoke. "Spike is really cool. My friends at school think he is weird. I mean 'weird' in a cool way, not, you know, a 'weird' way."

"What does that mean?" Isaac's father remained unconvinced. He was talking louder and, without realizing it, took off his glasses and started to clean them with his shirt, which he always did when he was upset. But, the family ignored him, which they always did when he became upset.

Mrs. Sanders played the role of referee. "Well," she

suggested, "perhaps we could invite Leonard and his parents to dinner tomorrow?" Her head nodded as if to magically make everything better through the invitation and get her husband to agree.

"And his *mom*," Isaac corrected his mother. "Spike lives with his *mom*. Not his parents."

"Awesome," screamed Rebecca. "He's coming to Hawaii with us! I'll go if, ah," she paused, "if he goes!"

"Oh no, you too?" asked Mr. Sanders, looking at Rebecca.

Rebecca thought Spike looked cool with his baggy jeans and his black, skull T-shirt. Besides his signature hair-do, Spike always wore a black, skull T-shirt. It was his "look," Isaac explained, irritated that his parents obviously did not "get it." Mr. Sanders absolutely did not "get it," looking worriedly back and forth from son to daughter.

~~~

"And so that is how Spike joined the Sanders family on their Hawaiian vacation," explained the old man to his grandson. The young boy had protested repeatedly, saying that he did not want to hear any stories. But, the old man ignored the complaining and continued reading the story. Andrew scowled and looked away. Every one of grandfather's visits included a new story, much to Andrew's dismay.

"Come on, Grandpa, there is no way that such an uptight family would let such a 'rad' kid come with them to Hawaii."

Andrew shook his head from side to side, trying to look disinterested in the story. At least he had turned his head momentarily to look at his grandfather, something Grandpa noticed but did not comment on.

"I thought you didn't want to hear my story," teased his grandfather, peeking over the reading glasses perched on the end of his large, crooked nose. He was reading from a book that looked as old as the reader. Andrew smiled as he imagined the pages of the book would, at any moment, fall out of the binding and splay across the floor. He made himself a bet that the book's torn cover would not last past the fourth chapter. "Well, do you," continued his grandfather. "Do you want to hear whether Spike went to Hawaii or not?"

Andrew hesitated before answering. He was still imagining the pages falling out of the book. "What a kick that would be!" He thought to himself. "And, it would get me out of this stupid story."

"Well, I don't," Andrew responded softly. "It's just. Well, you know, it's just that your stories aren't very realistic, Grandpa."

Setting the old book down on his lap, Grandpa continued, "Realistic! If you think that is so, then you are never going to believe the terrible fate that awaited Spike in Hawaii." Andrew's grandpa smiled, paused, then repeated the word: "Terrible." He added a slight quiver to his voice. It had the desired effect. Andrew was now paying attention. The old man continued, "To this day, I still have trouble believing it.

Now, where was I? The family flew to Hawaii the next month and the boy – what was his name?"

"Isaac," frowned Andrew, forgetting that he was not supposed to be paying attention to the story. "Geez, Grandpa, come on. You just said his name – only a minute ago. Are you really reading from that old book or just making this thing up?"

The old man ignored the comment and continued. "Oh yes, I remember. So, Isaac and his family, along with the two friends, Spike and Gabrielle…" But Andrew again interrupted his grandfather.

"*Grace*, Grandpa, not Gabrielle. *Grace* was her name!" Andrew rolled his eyes. How could his grandfather not remember the girl's name? Well, he was really old. Andrew again forgot that he was trying to show his grandfather that he did not want to hear yet another one of his stories and in the process missed the sly smile that crossed his grandfather's lips.

"You're making this story up as you go, aren't you, Grandpa?"

"Right, Grace was the girl. What did I say her name was? Anyway," continued the old man, his blue eyes sparkling with mischievousness. "Grace and the rest of them boarded the largest airplane any of them had ever seen, not knowing the perils that lie ahead…"

Chapter 2

Luau

Their first day in Hawaii had been perfect. The snow-white sand and warm, welcoming waters of Hapuna Beach made Isaac really feel as though he had discovered paradise. It was as if the poster hanging in his room at home had come to life.

Popping up from below the surface of the clear, blue-green water, Isaac exhaled. His strong blast of air blew a spout of water three feet straight up and free from his snorkel.

"Whew!"

He ripped the mask off his face and smiled a goofy grin from ear to ear. Waving to his mother, Isaac began babbling non-stop about the colorful fish he had just seen and the remarkable visibility under the water. "It looks like a big aquarium, Mom. I'm swimming in a big aquarium!" His mother waved back but, over the roar of the surf, could not hear a word her son said. She did, however, get the gist of what he was saying. She also snapped the perfect photograph.

Sitting on the beach towel, Isaac looked through the photographs his mother had taken. He had to laugh at the picture of himself standing in three feet of water, holding his snorkeling mask high overhead and snot dripping from his nose. "Nice photo," his sister and Grace teased. The next picture showed Rebecca and Grace standing under an arching palm tree bent toward the water like a stately hula dancer swaying to her own island beat. Mrs. Sanders commented that the two girls looked like hula dancers. Isaac agreed but changed the topic, saying that he liked these palms even better than the ones back home in Florida.

Though he loved the beach, Isaac always had the feeling that, after a few hours, he was ready for a shower and some shade. But not today. Isaac spent the entire day in the sand and surf. Even when the family packed up the car to head back to their hotel, he was already counting down the hours until he could go back to Hapuna Beach. Giddy with excitement, Isaac informed everyone that he wanted to go back to the same beach again and snorkel some more.

During the car ride to the hotel, Isaac imagined himself becoming a famous marine biologist who studied coral reefs and tropical fish. He even fancied himself discovering a new species of shark! Professor Isaac, the famous adventurer and biologist, would wrestle with the shark with his bare arms, tag it, and then release it. All the while, his film crew would catch the action for a nationally televised special! "Yes," Isaac thought to himself, "that is what I am going to do when I grow up!" He even started thinking about the name of his television show but was interrupted by Spike.

Spike seemed far less enamored of the day at the beach. He was listening to his headphones again, flailing his arms like an air guitarist. The power chord Spike played on his imaginary guitar hit Isaac solidly on his shoulder.

"Geez," thought Isaac. "Give it a rest." He would never say this out loud for fear of offending Spike, but for the life of him he could not imagine how Spike had not enjoyed the snorkeling. Spike had spent much of the day on his back, laying in the shade of a tree and listening to his headphones.

Back at the hotel, the family showered and dressed for what Mrs. Sanders said would be a very special evening. Isaac and the girls were excited and hurried to get ready. Spike simply rolled his eyes and took his grand time getting ready. Mrs. Sanders slipped out of the room to purchase tickets for the surprise evening. But, she could not keep the secret. The moment she returned to the suite of rooms, she blurted out that the whole family and their two guests were going to attend an authentic Hawaiian dinner and dance show.

After a sun-filled afternoon at the beach, the Sanders family arrived at the luau both glowing with their new tans and starving! The water always had a way of making Isaac feel like he had not eaten in days. He was ready to feast! They were attending their first Hawaiian luau and Mrs. Sanders even wore the colorful floral lei she was given at the airport the day prior when they arrived on the island. The luau grove was on the grounds of the hotel, nestled between two small stands of coconut trees a short walk from the beach. Dancers wearing Hawaiian grass skirts and decorative puka-shell necklaces handed each arriving guest fragrant leis made of yellow and white plumeria flowers, while the pulse of island drums pounded rhythmically from the stage in the distance.

~~~

"Aloha!" said an attractive hula dancer, her warm smile making Isaac blush with a curious mix of embarrassment and enchantment.

She seemed to notice and looked directly at Isaac, saying, "Welcome to Hawaii! In Hawaiian we say 'e komo mai' for welcome." She placed a lei around his neck.

Next came Rebecca and Grace, who received their leis from a muscular Hawaiian man whose arms and chest were lined with thick, darkly etched tattoos. The girls giggled with embarrassment when the man kissed Mrs. Sanders on the cheek after placing a flower lei around her neck. "You go, Mom," exclaimed Rebecca. Mrs. Sanders' tan immediately turned a bright shade of red. Noticing the amusement the kiss generated, the big Hawaiian performer winked playfully at both Rebecca and Grace. He then turned to Isaac and said in a deep voice, "You want a kiss too, Little Bruddah?"

The whole group roared with laughter, as Isaac took a step back and shook his head, "No way!" The big man's stomach rolled with each powerful laugh. He held out a fat fist in Isaac's direction and the boy gave his new friend a fist bump. The big fellow introduced himself as "Kalani."

"Now, Little Bruddah, le'me show you da way we do it in Hawaii." Kalani's big fist opened on both ends, with his pinky finger sticking out to one side and a meaty thumb sticking out in the opposite direction. "You do it," he said to the whole family. Everyone made a fist with their pinkies and thumbs straight out to either side. Kalani fluttered his outstretched pinky and thumb back and forth in rapid motion like a butterfly's wings. The whole family followed suit. Kalani playfully inspected each fist. "Now you know how to do da 'shakah.' This means you're Hawaiian!"

"Cool, thanks," said Isaac.

"Mahalo," smiled Kalani. "Mahalo means 'thanks' in Hawaiian," the big man explained.

"Mahalo," repeated Isaac.

"Mahalo," cheered Rebecca and Grace, nearly in perfect unison. "Well then, mahalo it is," nodded Isaac's mother somewhat awkwardly. She was still smiling from the kiss.

"Lame," the whisper came from behind Isaac. It was Spike.

It was the same thing he said yesterday at the airport when the hula dancers offered him a lei. Spike was the last in line after exiting the airplane and therefore the last to be offered a lei. "What is that thing?" he questioned while rolling his eyes with disgust.

"It's a lei. You're supposed to wear it around your neck," said the lady, bending down to place it around Spike's head.

"No way I'm wearing that garbage. That's messed up," complained Spike. Isaac was embarrassed, but not nearly as much as his mother. The hula dancer who had welcomed them at the airport pulled back in surprise, visibly offended by Spike's comments.

"I love my lei. Thanks, Ma'am," interjected Isaac's father, trying to smooth an uncomfortable scene. "Come along everyone." Mr. Sanders motioned in the direction of the baggage carousel. As the family turned and headed to pick up their luggage, Isaac caught his father glaring at Spike.

When Isaac looked at Spike, his friend scowled and said, "You're not going to wear that thing, are you? It's lame." Isaac removed his lei and dropped it into a garbage can that he happened to be walking by. Isaac's heart pounded with mixed emotions and he felt his face flush warm. He wanted to wear the lei, but he didn't want to disappoint his friend. " 'Course not," he muttered. " 'Course not," he repeated under his breath.

"Boys," said Mrs. Sanders in a stern voice, "I want good behavior on this trip." The concern Isaac's mother and father had expressed when they first learned their son wanted Spike to join them on vacation was still very apparent. Although they eventually stopped trying to talk their son into picking another one of his friends, they were never comfortable with the new boy in the school, one who was a full year older than their son. And they were especially uncomfortable with him traveling with the family.

As they walked down the long hallway of the airport concourse, Mr. Sanders reminded everyone but looked directly at Spike. "In Hawaii, it's a very special custom to welcome guests with leis," he explained, trying to mask his growing anger. He removed his glasses and cleaned them with the bottom of his un-tucked shirt, something he did when he was upset. Isaac noticed the gesture.

The two girls darted ahead toward the baggage carousel. "Hurry!" they shrieked. Nothing more was said, as everyone rushed to keep up with the two eager girls.

~~~

"Well, there's no way I'd wear a lei," proclaimed Andrew, interrupting his grandfather's story. "That's for girls."

"Not in Hawaii," corrected his grandfather. "It says that here in my old book."

"Yea, but I'm not Hawaiian. And, it is still for girls, Hawaiian or not."

Andrew's grandfather sighed, looking around the bedroom at posters of superheroes and spaceships. He murmured under his breath, "I suppose you think Kalani is girly or that you'd tell Kalani he was girly, huh?" But, before Andrew, who was speechless at the thought of having to face the 275-pound Kalani, could answer, the grandfather coughed to clear his voice and continued with the story…

~~~

Before the attractive hula dancer at the hotel's luau could put the lei around Spike's neck, the defiant boy raised an open hand. "Don't even think about it. It's enough that I'm even going to this stupid dance!" Unlike the embarrassed girl at the airport who had tried to give Spike a lei, this dancer seemed hardly to notice. She casually turned and smiled at Isaac's father. It seems she had encountered this resistance before, probably from other young boys.

Spike was small for his age but made up for his diminutive size with exaggerated confidence and the vocabulary and experiences of an older boy. These experiences came courtesy of having a much older brother who had run afoul of the law more than once. Spike grew up being terrorized by his older brother but saw how that bullying seemed to result in the respect of many of his peers and certainly of the children Spike's age. Spike thus adopted his brother's mannerisms and vocabulary. Surprisingly, it seemed to work at school. Students thought he was tough and let him alone.

"I'll take one," said Mr. Sanders, beaming in anticipation of getting a lei and obviously enjoying the attention of the young dancer. He nervously fidgeted with his glasses as the woman with the long, shimmering black hair gave him a kiss on the cheek after she fixed the flowers around his shoulders. The lei clashed mightily with the loud Hawaiian shirt, but Mr. Sanders did not mind in the least. "Eeww! Dad!" shrieked Rebecca at the site of her father smiling and standing still as if to wait for another kiss. She dragged out the word "Dad" into two syllables. Everyone laughed. Everyone, that is, except Isaac. He was upset...

Isaac felt torn between trying to impress his friend and doing what he really wanted to do. He had been excited to go to the luau even though, while getting ready in the room, he had pretended that he did not to want to attend because Spike complained about having to watch a "sissy dance." Spike had wanted to watch television instead and protested the whole way to the luau, but Isaac's parents were insistent that everyone go to the show. Mrs. Sanders explained in her motherly tone, "We can't leave you here alone, Leonard, er, ah, I mean Spike."

Spike shuffled along to the luau but refused to wear the matching Hawaiian shirts that Mrs. Sanders bought for everyone. Instead, he wore his trademark black, skull T-shirt and gelled his hair into an outrageous spike running down the middle of his head. As they walked to the luau, Mr. Sanders glanced at Spike and whispered to his wife, "I guess that is the new Hawaiian look." Even Isaac smiled at the joke, but quickly regained his disinterested composure.

As a photographer snapped photos of all the guests

wearing leis, Spike grabbed Isaac's arm, nodding with his head to the back of the luau grounds. He obviously wanted to get away from the dancers and get into the seating. "Come on, who needs this?" Isaac turned and started to follow Spike, reaching up to remove his own lei. But, just as he did, he heard a husky voice from behind him.

"No problem, Little Bruddah. You can wear da lei. It is *cool*." It was Kalani. He emphasized the word cool with an exaggerated wink, but somehow Kalani did make it cool. Then he grinned and added, "But, da Skinny Bruddah here, his hair is too pointy for leis." Kalani was holding his big hands on top of his head and pointing his fingers straight up toward the sky, imitating Spike's spiky hair. "Dat hair will cut da lei to pieces!"

Kalani roared with laughter and Isaac managed a discreet smile.

"Puh-lease," Spike nearly spit out the words. But Spike's cool was beginning to fail as he looked up at the big Hawaiian.

Kalani winked at Spike, "Or maybe da flowers too heavy for you, Bruddah?" Spike was, after all, as thin as the spikes of hair atop his head and a half a head shorter than Isaac.

Isaac felt emboldened by the big Hawaiian. "No, let's stay," he said to his friend, waving his hand causally toward the dancers. But when Spike looked at Isaac with disappointment, Isaac waffled, offering a weak explanation: "I mean, my parents already paid for this luau. It was really expensive."

"Come on boys," said Mr. Sanders, putting his hands behind both boys' backs and pushing them forward. "They're getting ready to take the pig out of the underground oven. That should be…*cool*," Isaac's father scrunched up his face to imitate Spike. "Yeah, real cool," mocked Spike back.

"Later, Little Bruddahs," yelled Kalani. When Isaac turned to wave goodbye, Kalani signed back with the Hawaiian 'shakah' but then quickly moved his waving hand to the top of his head, spreading his fingers to make fun of Spike's hair. As Kalani winked, Isaac smiled back. "Kalani is really funny," thought Isaac.

He was glad he was at the luau.

Chapter 3

🍹

Malama

"**L**ook!" pointed Grace. An elderly woman with wild, flowing reddish hair containing sprouts of gray and white, stood on a raised stage beside the underground oven. Nightfall had come quickly on the island. The darting shadows of nearby torches dancing across the woman's face gave her a ghostly appearance. As she spoke, Isaac found himself staring at her hair, which to him looked like the flames of a volcano erupting around her.

There was something eerie but alluring about the mistress of the ceremony as she described how they prepared the pig and feast for the luau. The men referred to the round, old woman as "The Malama," and Isaac heard Kalani call her "Malamalama."

Two shirtless Hawaiian men, their backs glistening in sweat, removed what looked like burned garbage bags from a hole in the ground. In a wavering but husky voice that seemed too low for a woman, the old lady informed the gathering audience that the men were removing ti leaves from a plant that grew around the island. The underground oven, Isaac learned, was called an "imu." The pig, Malama said, was called a "pua'a," and it would be on the menu at the luau's grand buffet.

"Eeww!" screamed Rebecca. "Gross."

Spike agreed, "Looks like garbage! Don't they have a McDonald's here?"

"Everything looks like garbage to you!" scolded Grace angrily.

While Rebecca was still somewhat excited by having the "cool" kid from school traveling with them, her friend Grace had tired of Spike by the time they checked in on the first plane to Hawaii.

Mrs. Sanders intervened to tell the kids that the luau had plenty of food for everyone's tastes. Spike murmured something inaudible, but Mrs. Sanders pretended not to hear him.

A bellowing horn pierced the air and grabbed the guests' attention. The sound came from a large conch shell. Kalani was standing in the center of the stage holding the shell in two hands, his massive chest heaving as he blew into the shell. A second blast of the conch beckoned the tourists to depart from the underground oven and move to the luau grounds. Isaac found himself wanting to run to get one of the seats near the front of the stage, but Spike shuffled slowly a few paces behind the family. The slow pace was driving Isaac crazy and he had trouble restraining his excitement. They passed rows of palm trees that lined the entrance to the luau grounds like tall soldiers. A large tiki hut with a thatched roof made of palm fronds sat off to one side. The sides of the hut were open and it contained a flat, stone stage that extended a distance out from the hut and nearly into the audience. To the sides of the stage were sprawling trees whose shoots and limbs stretched like a giant octopus. They were among the biggest trees Isaac had ever seen.

"A toast," the mistress of ceremonies raised a glass. "This pig is a sacred gift from Madam Pele." The old woman with the flaming hair did not speak the words. No, it was more a chant – a haunting, wavering chant. She raised a glass of gin and poured the entire contents down her throat in one gulp. All the tourists held up their fruity island cocktails and repeated the salute. Isaac raised his island fruit punch with a big smile. His mother led their table in a toast to the start of their Hawaiian vacation.

Spike frowned and whispered to Isaac, "Don't they have Coke at this place?" Isaac did not answer but sheepishly lowered his cup of fruit punch to the table. "I can't believe you drank that lame drink," said Spike rolling his eyes at his friend.

Before Isaac could answer, a large hand came to rest on his shoulder. It was Kalani. With his other hand he reached across the table, grabbed Spike's island punch, and raised it high over his head. "To Malamalama!" His voice boomed like a brass tuba. Like the old lady he saluted, Kalani threw the entire contents of the drink down his throat in one great swallow. "Ahhhh! Now that's one tasty drink, Bruddahs!" With the back of his forearm, Kalani wiped clean the red circle around his mouth. Isaac laughed as he watched Kalani run back toward the stage. He was beginning to think Kalani was the funniest person he had ever met!

The Sanders family ended up sitting on the side of the luau grounds, in the shadows of the surrounding coconut grove and sprawling banyan tree. Their seats were not in the front, but they were not too far back – despite Spike's slow shuffling on the way in to the luau – and they could see the stage well enough. Countless Hawaiian torches lit the luau grounds and the dim lighting and presence of fire added to the excitement everyone felt. It was a comfortably warm and clear evening with a slight breeze. The sky featured a show of stars worthy of the best planetariums. In short, Isaac thought it was a perfect night.

"E komo mai," sang Kalani, the silhouette of his thick body framed by a single spotlight. Kalani was so big that it seemed the spotlight was not large enough to capture his image. He was well over six feet tall and looked as wide too. Kalani continued, "In Hawaiian, welcome. Welcome, Bruddahs and Sistahs, to our show, The Magical Islands of the Pacific."

Suddenly, a symphony of pulsating drums thundered through the luau grounds. Without realizing it, Isaac and his sister were rocking back and forth to the catchy beat. Another spotlight highlighted three musicians, one pounding a thudding base drum and the other two playing what looked like wooden logs of varying sizes. The jet-black hair of the middle and main drummer flew wildly as he bounced his head to the beat. Isaac's mother reached over and squeezed his arm with excitement.

"This is really cool," Isaac thought to himself. He didn't dare share his thought with Spike.

Kalani lept off the stage and, still mirrored by the main spotlight, ran through the audience. He ended up directly behind the table where Isaac and his family were sitting. Though powerfully built and covered in tattoos, Kalani had soft eyes. His smile was infectious and it was impossible not to smile back at Kalani. Another blast from Kalani's conch shell produced from the shadows a small Hawaiian man, perhaps in his early twenties, holding a machete high above his head. Rebecca and Grace gasped, and Isaac's mother squeezed his arm a second time. As quickly as he appeared, the limber man swung the machete from side to side then clenched it between his teeth. His hands free, he started climbing the coconut tree.

More than climbing the tree, the man seemed to hop up the tree like an animal that spent its whole life living in the tree. A rope, tied around his feet helped him hold tightly to the tree. He bounded upward at an astounding pace. Both feet pushed along the tree in unison like a kangaroo running vertically.

"Look at that!" Isaac exclaimed, elbowing Spike. Even Spike forgot that he was trying to act tough. His wide-open mouth revealed his true emotions. Mrs. Sanders repeated her son's comment: "Look at that!" she shrieked.

"Watch, and you will learn." The voice sent a shiver up Isaac's spine. It came from directly behind him. Light hands rested like feathers from a breeze on Isaac's shoulders. Turning around, Isaac gasped momentarily when he saw that it was the old lady from the show. Her eyes gazed upward at the climber. She repeated herself in a low, raspy voice. "Watch, and you will learn."

She was wearing a flowing, reddish-orange dress with a black print of prehistoric Hawaiian carvings. She smelled of the earth, not unlike the sweet smell of soil when Isaac helped his mother plant a garden, and she seemed almost ghost-like in her sudden appearance. Isaac glanced back up to the top of the coconut tree – the man had already climbed to the top of the tree. The rope between his feet must be the key, thought Isaac. Then Isaac glanced back behind him again. "Perhaps this is what she wanted me to learn," he thought. But the old lady had stepped backward into the shadows of the trees; rather, she seemed to float back into the darkness.

"Strange," whispered Isaac. "Who is she?" he pondered. A voice deep inside him asked, "Not who, but *what* is she?"

Isaac looked quickly at his sister, parents, Grace, and then Spike to see if they noticed the woman. If they did, they did not show it. All of them were staring at the man shining in the spotlight at the top of the tree. Long palms stretched over his head and swayed in the gentle breeze. The light from the torches below stretched upward and flickered on the underside of the palm leaves, giving them the appearance of moving much more than they were. Holding onto the tree with one hand, the man raised the machete and swung it at one of the larger coconuts. "WHACK!" At the very moment the machete struck, the drumming stopped.

Like a heavy brown football, the coconut dropped toward the ground. A collective gasp came from the audience, including a loud, wheezing sound by Spike that was easily heard over the sudden silence. Rebecca reflexively jumped backward, out of her chair and nearly into Isaac's lap.

Just as the speeding coconut was about to hit the ground, Kalani reached out and caught it. Or rather, the coconut seemed to fall right into his large hands. The audience applauded wildly. And that quickly, the old lady again appeared in the spotlight. In her thick voice she explained how Hawaiians could husk the seemingly impenetrable coconut with only a large stick. While the rest of his table seemed only casually interested in how Kalani husked the coconut, Isaac found the demonstration amazing. He took Malama's advice and watched closely in order to learn how it was done.

Next to Kalani, sticking up from the ground, was a four-foot-high stake, sharpened at the top. After holding the coconut above his head long enough to build the suspense, the big Hawaiian brought it down with a powerful swoop on top of the stake, impaling it a few inches in. This time it was Isaac's turn to gasp, which seemed to catch Kalani's attention. After a quick wink at Isaac, Kalani then twisted the coconut sideways and the shell gave way. With a quick jerk, he raised the fruit above his head as the coconut milk spilled down into his open mouth and across his broad chest.

Kalani raised the two halves of the coconut up, licked his lips, and roared, "In Hawaiian, we say 'ono'! That means deee-licious!" The audience applauded.

"And now, we begin the show." The words came from the old lady, now standing on the stage in the spotlight. "How did she manage to get to the stage so fast," said Isaac out loud, not aware that he did so. "Huh?" answered his mother, seeming not to notice either the question or Malama.

"This is really cool," Isaac thought to himself. Forgetting his hesitancy and the snide remarks from Spike, Isaac lost himself in the show.

The show was fast-paced and featured a variety of songs and dances from different Pacific Island countries. Halfway into the performance, the old woman announced that the dancers needed volunteers to join them on stage. Grace's hand immediately shot high into the air, as she screamed "Me, me. Pick me!" Others in the audience also waved their hands about, while some people seemed to try and melt backward into their chairs to hide. Isaac's mother was one of them, flatly informing those at their table that they were not to let the dancers pick her. Isaac wasn't sure exactly how he was supposed to prevent the dancers from picking his mother. But rather than explain that to her, he decided it would be both fun and funny to see her dance.

"Why would anyone want to do that?" Spike was shaking his body comically, trying to imitate the dancers and making fun of the show. "Gee, I'm Hawaiian, look at me…" He looked appropriately goofy shaking on his chair. He even stuck out his tongue like the male dancers had done in one of the war dances from the island of New Zealand. But, in mid-sentence, Spike was lifted out of his seat. A great paw dropped like a construction crane and scooped the boy up into the air. It was Kalani.

"We got a volunteer here, Aunty," Kalani grinned while announcing his 'catch' to the old lady. The audience roared with laughter at the site of the giant carrying Spike, like a loaf of bread, with one arm to the stage. Spike flailed his arms and kicked his legs, but it had absolutely no effect.

"You too, Little Sistah," Kalani nodded his head to Grace, who eagerly jumped out of her chair and ran to the stage. Two men, two women, and another girl near Rebecca and Grace's age were also led to the stage by the dancers.

"Ha, serves him right!" Isaac's father was leaning far back in his chair laughing. He quite enjoyed watching Spike trying to wriggle free… with no success.

"Now, John," scolded Mrs. Sanders. But she was only partly serious.

When Kalani finally set Spike down on stage, Isaac

thought his friend would really let the big fellow and old lady have it with a string of sarcastic words. Perhaps even a few of the curse words Spike had learned from his older brother. That is what happened at school in March when their school librarian, Ms. Janson, told Spike to be quiet. Spike's outburst made Isaac and his classmates uncomfortable, but it was yet another incident that enhanced Spike's growing reputation as a tough kid not to be messed with despite his slight size.

But, rather than react angrily, Spike seemed to freeze on stage. He said nothing. He did not move. Not even a blink.

Isaac thought the whole incident was hilarious. He agreed with his father that Spike probably deserved to be embarrassed. But then, suddenly, Malama leaned down and whispered something into Spike's ear. Isaac knew his friend well enough to know that whatever she said bothered him because the blood seemed to drain from Spike's face. It was replaced by an expression Isaac had never seen from Spike before. Spike looked bewildered and lost as he gazed up at the old woman. "I wonder what she said?" thought Isaac.

Kalani ended the awkward moment by showing the tourists on stage how to dance. They all moved enthusiastically but uncomfortably on stage. Grace was the best of the lot. Spike was the worst. He hardly moved.

"Need more hips in your dance, Bruddah, if you want to be Hawaiian," Kalani announced to the audience while looking straight at Spike. The laughter unfroze Spike, who promptly ran off the stage and straight back to the hotel room.

"Maybe he had too much pua'a pig!" suggested Kalani, putting his hand over his enormous, round rear end and acting as if he was about to go to the bathroom. The audience was nearly crying themselves with laughter. Isaac too found the whole incident amusing, but stood and followed Spike back to the room. Kalani observed Isaac leave and gave him a quick 'shaka.' Isaac returned the gesture. He hated to leave, but…

~~~

"Grandpa, what did the old lady say to Spike?" Andrew had long since stopped pretending that he did not want a story before bedtime.

Earlier that night, Andrew would have done anything to get out of having to hear another story from his grandfather. In fact, when his grandfather announced to the whole family in the living room that he would tuck the boy into bed and tell him a short story, Andrew even told his mother that he was tired and needed to get some sleep because of a spelling test in school the next day.

Of course, Andrew's mother knew a whopper when she heard one. Since when did her son ever want to go to sleep? She smiled at her father and told him that Andrew loved his bedtime stories. Andrew shot his mother an angry look as if to say "Mom, don't you dare. Not another story from Grandpa!" As he walked up the steps behind his grandfather, Andrew even mouthed to his mother the word "H-E-L-P."

"Grandpa, what did the old lady say to Spike?" he again asked, not really caring if his grandfather told him.

"Now, hold on," his grandfather explained. "I'll tell you."

"You see," the old man explained, his voice dropping as he leaned forward toward the bed where Andrew was supposed to be sleeping. "The old lady knew his real name. She called him Leonard."

"But, how would she know that?" asked Andrew.

"Well, that is the point. She also told Leonard that he would upset the gods if he continued to be so disrespectful. You see, the Hawaiian gods demand respect, especially Madam Pele, the goddess of fire and volcanoes. The same was true of the spirit of the great King Kamehameha!"

"Tell me about King Kame..." Andrew had trouble pronouncing the name, but his face was lit up with excitement.

Grandpa ignored the comment for a minute, stretching his tired legs and rubbing his large, crooked nose, one that had obviously been badly broken at some earlier point in his life.

"Well," he continued in a matter-of-fact tone. "Kamehameha was the first Hawaiian king. In Hawaii they call it 'ali'i.' He was a giant man. Six-and-a-half feet tall and powerful. He had been born on the Big Island of Hawaii not far from the exact spot where Isaac was watching the luau. He later conquered all the other islands. Some Hawaiians felt that King Kamehameha's spirit still watched over the island.

So, if you do not respect the Hawaiian gods and ali'i, they get very angry and bad things happen."

"Really?" Andrew was now sitting up in bed.

"Well, not really," his grandfather grinned, leaning back in his chair. "But who knows?" He left the thought hanging.

He continued, explaining how Isaac had trouble sleeping that night. Isaac thought about why Malama had singled him out and told him to watch and learn from the coconut tree-climbing performance and the husking of the coconut. He also wondered whether he could climb a coconut tree. It also bothered him that no one else seemed to notice that the old woman had talked to him. During one of the dances at the luau, for example, Isaac leaned over and whispered to his mother, asking her if she had heard the old woman speak to him. Isaac's mother quickly shook her head in the negative, again squeezed his arm gently, and went back to watching the dance. His sister did the same.

When sleep finally overcame Isaac, sometime well past midnight, he slept fitfully. Dreams of the old woman, her wild, fire-like hair, and pounding drums played hauntingly in his head. The old woman named Malamalama appeared to Isaac as a spirit in various forms. Spike also seemed to have trouble sleeping, for he tossed and turned all night as well.

"Well, young man, I think that is enough for tonight," Andrew's grandfather gently closed the book and removed his glasses. "You mentioned something earlier about a spelling test in school. So, you better get your rest. We'll continue tomorrow night because the story takes a turn for the worse the next day. You see, the most terrible tsunami ever to hit the islands strikes. That night would be the last night on this earth for many of the people at that luau. Goodnight, Andrew."

Andrew reached out and grabbed his grandfather's arm. "No, Grandpa. You have to continue. Please."

"Alright then," said the grandfather, noting that this was the first time Andrew ever wanted a story read. "Just a little more...one more chapter," he agreed.

Chapter 4

Surprise

Ring! Ring! Ring! Clara Sanders picked up the phone. She was more asleep than awake and still feeling the effects of the change in time zones and the "jet lag." The flight across the country was long. So was the flight across the Pacific Ocean to the Big Island.

"Aloha and good morning," said the operator on the other end of the line.

"Rise and shine," Mrs. Sanders groaned to a room full of zombies. No one stirred.

The excitement of what Mrs. Sanders had planned for the family helped get her out of bed and dressed. Isaac and Spike lay in strange zig-zag formation on two, small roll-out beds, while Rebecca and Grace shared a bed in the opposite end of the suite, with Rebecca sleeping with her head where her feet belonged.

Mr. Sanders groped blindly for his glasses on the nightstand beside his bed. "What time is it?" he yawned.

"Today I have an incredible surprise for everyone," answered Clara Sanders. "We're taking a tour to the other side of the Big Island to visit Kilauea, the world's most active volcano!"

Only Isaac responded to his mother's announcement, sitting up in bed groggily and rubbing his eyes. "Cool, mom," he croaked in his "morning voice."

Mrs. Sanders told her husband to go to the front desk and pick up the rental car. She then called to order room service for everyone.

The hotel room was tastefully decorated with a casual elegance. But the design left no question about the location of the hotel. Everything from the paintings on the walls to the design of the wallpaper to the bedspreads said "Hawaii!" Colorful tropical flowers sat on the center table and two small palms filled pots on either side of the door.

"What does everyone want for breakfast?" she asked. Mrs. Sanders picked up the clothing and pillows that littered the room while she talked.

"Coffee. Black," her husband managed as he dressed.

"You know, Hawaii is supposed to have the best coffee in the world," Mrs. Sanders smiled. "It's grown here in Kona. The secret, they say, is the rich lava soil."

"Well, then, make it Kona coffee... but hold the lava!" Mr. Sanders managed a joke while he walked into the bathroom.

Before going into the bathroom he turned on the lights in the room. "Get up kids."

Each of the kids sleepily told Mrs. Sanders what they wanted for breakfast, starting with Isaac, who ordered French toast with blueberries. He heard his mother laugh, then cover the receiver of the phone before saying to him, "The operator says they serve it with pineapple and guava syrup." Mrs. Sanders licked her lips, indicating that she thought it sounded good. Isaac smiled, remembered the word Kalani used at the luau the night before for delicious, and said "Ono!" Rebecca blurted out her usual order: bacon and eggs. Grace yelled that she wanted waffles with sausage. Mrs. Sanders was always on a diet so she ordered cereal and fruit. "My guess is that it will be pineapple," she said giggling while muffling her words so the operator could not hear her.

Isaac spoke out loud, saying he thought French toast with pineapple and guava syrup sounded exotic. "Go for it," said his dad. And Isaac did. Spike did not answer. He was still in bed with a pillow over his head. When Mrs. Sanders again asked him what he wanted for breakfast, Spike murmured something that sounded like the word "sleep."

"Sorry, Spike, that's not on the menu," Mr. Sanders smiled, winking at Isaac. Isaac smiled back but covered his mouth with his hand so that Spike wouldn't hear him giggling. "Clara, get Spike French toast too…" Mr. Sanders suggested as he closed the bathroom door behind him.

No one mentioned the incident the night before, when

Spike ran back to the room. Isaac had joined his friend back in the room, but in the morning he regretted not staying for the rest of the luau. The two simply sat quietly watching television until they fell asleep.

Breakfast was delicious. Isaac was really getting to like this Pacific paradise and he could not wait to go to the volcano. While he was packing his backpack – binoculars, water bottles, camera, notepad, flashlight, granola bars, and his all-purpose pen – he said to Spike, "Come on, get dressed. My father will be back any minute."

Spike had managed to at least sit up in bed, although his notorious spiky hair was now sideways. He didn't touch his food.

Thirty minutes later the door opened and Mr. Sanders came into the room. "Guess what?" He was smiling ear-to-ear. "I rented a large jeep. It's even tan – looks like the kind they use on a safari!"

"Cool!" Isaac stood and prepared to give his father a high five.

"Lame," Spike intoned. Isaac caught himself and stopped before slapping his father's hand.

Mr. Sanders was obviously disappointed that his son was so worried about impressing and accommodating Spike. He knew Isaac had always wanted to ride in a jeep. But Isaac turned his eyes away from his father and toward his own feet, much as he had done after the terrible incident involving Rebecca a few years ago. Had he been looking, he would have seen the disappointment begin turning into anger, but his father then composed himself. Grinning, Mr. Sanders said to Spike, "Well, they did have an awesome family station wagon. I think it was white, but they said something about having a pink one in the lot too. I could always exchange the jeep!"

Isaac grinned and his sister and Grace giggled. "Very funny," groaned Spike.

"Let's go!" Mr. Sanders picked up the bags his wife had packed and started out the door. "Now, Spike." Mr. Sanders emphasized the word *now*, "Or I'll exchange the jeep for the pink tricycle."

"Spike," said Mrs. Sanders, with a worried expression on her face. "You haven't eaten a thing. You'll need your energy where we are going. The top of the volcano is a few thousand feet in elevation and there is a lot of hiking. We're going to explore an ancient lava tube as well and see the crater where one of the Hawaiian goddesses lives. You'll enjoy it."

"Can't wait," Spike said sarcastically as he shuffled to the bathroom with his clothes in his hand. Mrs. Sanders motioned for her son to pack an extra granola bar and one of the juices from the small refrigerator in the room for Spike. He did.

"Maybe I should pack another one for Madam Pele," laughed Isaac. "The news report last night said there was some minor rumbling at the volcano. Maybe she's hungry?"

"Well maybe she is, Isaac." Mrs. Sanders smiled.

~~~

"Man, Grandpa," complained Andrew, "Spike is really becoming a drag."

"You're tellin' me, Tiger," agreed his grandfather, without looking up from the old book. "Of course, you wouldn't 'hang out' with someone like him, would you?"

Andrew usually complained when his grandfather called him embarrassing nicknames like "Tiger" or "Sport." But, he did not notice it this time, boasting "Are you kiddin' me! I wouldn't be caught dead with that kid. I think Spike is the one who is L-A-M-E." He slowly spelled out the word to accentuate his point. "Me, I'd hang out with Bruddah Kalani!"

Andrew admitted that he thought Spike was kind of cool at first. But, he reasoned, there was something wrong with a kid who would not be excited about seeing a real, active volcano!

"Well," his grandfathered breathed, heavily. "If they knew what that volcano had in store for them, I doubt they would have gone."

Andrew laid back in bed, his eyes not leaving his grandfather's mouth as the old man continued the story.

Chapter 5

Volcano

Isaac had wanted to see his first Hawaiian rainbow, but the day was too perfect for the warm thunderstorm it would take to produce the island's natural fireworks. The sky glistened a bright blue, bluer even than the Florida skies Isaac was used to back home. The sun was already warm, despite the early hour. But the temperature was not too hot – a comfortable 82 degrees, made all the more pleasant by a slight breeze blowing off the ocean. As the family rounded the southern point of the Big Island and headed north to the southeast coast, the windward trades picked up slightly and helped cool down the coming of mid-day.

The family drove on the only major road around the island, which was nicknamed the "belt road" for good reason: It wrapped around the edge of the entire, huge island like a belt. The southern point of the Big Island was called "Ka'u" and Mr. Sanders told everyone that he read that it was the southernmost point in the United States.

Isaac interjected, saying that he thought Key West in their home state of Florida was the southernmost place. His father corrected him. Key West was only the most southern point in the *continental* United States. Ka'u was even farther south. "In fact," Mr. Sanders explained, "the strong ocean currents from Ka'u run straight southward and don't stop until Antarctica. So, you might not want to doze off while floating on a raft around here!" Normally, Isaac's father was used to his family not reacting to his goofy trivia. But this time both his wife and son responded.

"Cool," agreed Isaac, reaching into his backpack to get his camera. "Can we stop here to get a photo?"

"You bet," answered his father. "But, let's do it on the way back. How about we stop to eat dinner here? A southernmost dinner!" Mr. Sanders laughed at his own corny joke – something he frequently did by himself.

Spike mouthed the same words, while shaking his head in mock disgust. Isaac wanted to say that he liked the idea of having dinner in Ka'u, but he again stopped himself when Spike threw him a sideways glance, snickering at Mr. Sanders' corniness.

Isaac had always been rather adventurous. He enjoyed hiking and camping, and, like his mother, was always ready for new experiences. He had checked out books on volcanoes from his school library and a video from the local public library the week before their trip in order to learn more about them. Such inquisitiveness was typical for Isaac. He was also a rather resourceful kid, one who knew how to tie several different kinds of knots, fix his friends' bicycles, build a fire, read a compass, and so on. So, this day was really turning out to be an exciting one for him; he could not wait to visit a real, active volcano!

As they drove out of the small, southernmost town, and toward the Hawaii Volcanoes National Park, the traffic slowed, then came to a stop. Everyone leaned forward, as if to give themselves a better view. Isaac exhaled in disappointment. He was too excited to get to the volcano to be stuck in traffic. Spike also exhaled, but it was a disinterested sigh. He put his large, puffy headphones on and turned up the volume.

The line of cars began creeping forward. A man wearing a bright orange jump suit and holding a small red flag waved their jeep to the center of the road in order to give ample room as the vehicle went around an old mini-bus. A line of men shuffled into the bus. But this bus had bars across the windows and was painted all white. The dozen men in the line were wearing the same orange jump suit. A uniformed law enforcement officer stood watching the line of men, a shotgun resting on his shoulder. His eyes were undetectable behind the dark lenses of his sunglasses. The officer looked very serious, and Isaac and his family were glad of it because of what his father said next.

"Chain gang," announced Mr. Sanders.

"What's that?" asked Rebecca.

"Convicts. Prisoners," Mrs. Sanders replied for her husband. "They make them do work while they're in jail. Stuff like picking up trash and clearing away bushes and trees on the edge of the road, right honey?" She spoke to her husband. Her eyes, however, never left the site of the chain gang as she spoke and her voice sounded a bit uneasy.

"Yea, that's right. Convicts. Even here in paradise, it seems there are folks who do the wrong thing." Mr. Sanders slowed the vehicle.

One by one, the line of cars passed around the bus. As the Sanders family's jeep rounded the bus, Isaac saw a huge man entering the side door. When he stepped up onto the stairs on the bus, the whole mini-bus seemed to lean toward him. On the back of his jump suit were three large, black letters: HDC. Isaac's father answered his question before the boy could ask it. HDC stood for the Hawaii Department of Corrections. The sleeves of the jumpsuit were cut out, revealing thickly muscled arms that looked like hams hanging off the man's shoulders. The other convicts seemed to avoid him, keeping their distance... at least as much as was possible with another officer, this one holding a clipboard and giving orders, hurrying the men onto the bus.

The big man literally had to squeeze through the open door, glancing his shoulders sideways in order to fit into the bus. A swollen belly rubbed against the door as the man entered. As Isaac watched the brute, he sensed someone was watching him. And then their eyes met.

~~~

"Who? Who's eyes?" demanded Andrew of his grandfather.

"I'm getting to that," said his grandfather. The old man yawned. It was getting late.

"It was one of the prisoners, right?"

Andrew's grandfather nodded his head "yes" and told Andrew that it was not just one of the prisoners, it was the worst of the lot.

~~~

Staring at Isaac was the cruelest-looking face he had ever seen. The face seemed to be made more of leather than of flesh. One black eye stared straight into Isaac's face. The other eye was a cloudy, almost milky color and looked empty of expression. A scar stretched above and below that lifeless eye, running vertically from the forehead to the lower left jaw and across the tanned face. The man was the only one of the group who did not seem to shy away from the big brute who entered the bus. Rather, as the big man was stepping into the bus, the man with the scar – who was standing behind him – kicked him in the backside and yelled something that must have been funny, because a few of the other prisoners laughed. Theirs were not unrestrained laughs, but nervous chuckles that came out the sides of their mouths. It was obvious they did not want the brute to know they were laughing at him.

The guard with the clipboard said something to the man with the scar and then pointed at him. But, like those convicts laughing, he too seemed nervous and his pointing motion was more of a quick jerk than an outstretched gesture. That quickly, the officer, pencil still in hand, withdrew his arm and continued writing. He was obviously using a list to check off each convict at they entered the bus.

The man with the scar ignored the warning and, instead, looked directly at Isaac, whose face was pressed up against the jeep's window. The cold, black eye held Isaac's gaze for several seconds. Isaac's blue eyes widened. Then the uniformed guard with the shotgun shoved the man forward with the butt of the gun, growling "Move it, de Silva. You've got one good eye. Use it."

De Silva did not flinch. He maintained his stare at Isaac. Slowly, however, the edges of his mouth curled upward into a menacing grin. The eye finally blinked and the prisoner turned and boarded the bus. He was of slight height and built, not half the size of the behemoth that entered the prison bus before him. But he exuded a power. An intensity. Isaac watched the back of his shaved head disappear into the bus. And the man was gone.

As their jeep drove past the bus, Isaac felt a chill run up his spine. His body shuddered involuntarily and he blinked his eyes shut tight as if to try and forget the unnerving site of the convict.

~~~

Andrew's grandfather placed the old book in his lap. "Want to know what de Silva's first name was?" he asked the boy.

Andrew nodded his head once.

"Scar. That's what they called him." The grandfather explained that the nickname was for obvious reasons and that he did not know de Silva's real first name. "Seems he got into a fight with a rather large knife..."

"And lost," Andrew finished the sentence smartly.

"Well," paused the grandfather. "You wouldn't say that if you had seen what happened to the fellow holding the knife."

Andrew's eyes widened just like Isaac's had, and his mouth opened ever so slightly.

"It seems Scar knew that there was something worth knowing about Isaac, or that he and Isaac were destined to meet." Andrew's grandfather began talking without reading from the old text. His eyes shut as he leaned his head back. "Yes, Isaac too seemed to recognize that the encounter... ah, that they were going to meet." The old man left the word hanging for a moment before continuing. "And that stare meant something too."

"Anyway," Andrew's grandfather snapped out of his thoughts and continued. "The Sanders family and their two guests drove to the National Park to hike around the volcano."

"Grandpa," Andrew interrupted. "What about Scar? What did he know? How come he and Isaac would have to meet? I don't understand. And what about the giant man that entered the bus before Scar?" Andrew's excitement caused him to slur the words, blurring them together at a fast pace.

"Well, the giant – a good description, by the way, Andrew…" The old man was again speaking without reading, or without looking at his grandson. "His name was, get this," he paused and smiled, "Tiny."

"Tiny?" asked Andrew scrunching up his eyes as if to say "ridiculous."

"Yea, that is what they called him. Tiny. Of course, he was anything but… Biggest man I, err, ah, they ever saw. Probably six-feet-four, arms like legs, and a chest like a refrigerator."

"Wow," breathed Andrew. "That's big. Really big! What did Spike say?"

"Oh, he never even saw them. Had his eyes closed listening to his music." Andrew's grandfather yawned again and stood slowly, stretching his back. "That's enough for tonight." He patted Andrew on the top of the head and said "Goodnight, Tiger." Grandpa turned out the light, but before he closed the door, he said over his shoulder, "But Tiny was not the mean one. Not nearly as mean as Scar. He was the one to watch out for."

Andrew, much like Isaac after the luau, had trouble sleeping and his dreams were filled with images of swaying palm trees and a menacing eye staring at him.

Chapter 6

Quake

"**G**randpa, why did Isaac's parents allow Spike to go on their vacation? I mean, I can see why they let Grace come along with Rebecca...but Spike? No way!" Andrew motioned toward the door of his bedroom, then continued. "There is no way mom would allow me to bring someone like Spike on our family vacations. No way!" He dragged the word "no" out for five full seconds.

Andrew's grandfather explained that the family had suffered through a very frightening incident involving Rebecca about five years before the trip to Hawaii. Since then, Grace and Rebecca had become best of friends and Rebecca's family was so appreciative of Grace's friendship that they considered her to be a part of the family. Grace often slept over at the Sanders' home, joined the family on nights out, and even traveled with them. Mr. and Mrs. Sanders had not long before become concerned that Isaac might feel left out because he had not yet had a friend join the family on a vacation.

Obviously, Andrew's grandfather explained, Spike would not have been the first choice of Isaac's parents. Or the second or third. But it would not have been fair to Isaac to let Rebecca bring a friend and then not agree to Isaac doing the same.

~~~

Hawaii Volcanoes National Park sits on the windward side of the Big Island and contains the most active volcano on Earth – Kilauea. Since the early 1980s, Kilauea has been erupting almost continuously. However, unlike the explosive volcanic eruptions commonly seen on television or depicted in textbooks, this eruption is somewhat safe. In fact, tourists flock to the National Park to see the vast fields of ancient black lava, cratered landscape, countless steam vents, and the famous Halema'uma'u Crater, where Hawaiian legend suggests the goddess Madam Pele lives. But, the main attraction at Kilauea is the Pu'u O'o vent on the volcano's slope which emits a steady, slow gurgle of lava.

Although the heat of the lava keeps both tourists and scientists at a distance, it is possible to watch the lava ooze, much like a thick molasses or gooey syrup, down the sloping cliffs of the volcano toward the ocean. This constant lava flow has also had the effect of adding many acres of new land to the island, meaning that the Big Island is actually growing.

It was this famous lava flow that the Sanders family was preparing to see. Everyone was giddy with excitement as they entered the National Park. Everyone, that is, except Spike. He did not respond when Isaac bumped him on the arm, trying to get him to look at the sign welcoming them to the world's most active volcano. Isaac wanted a picture of himself standing beside the sign. Spike declined the invitation to have his picture taken but Rebecca climbed on Grace's back like a cheerleader and the two posed beside Isaac.

One of the sites Isaac most wanted to see was the ruins of a small town that had been buried by lava. Because of the slow rate at which Kilauea's lava flowed down the mountain, the residents had ample time to escape unharmed. In fact, many of the locals had sprayed water from hoses at the advancing bubbly mass. But this proved to be a futile effort, as nothing stops a volcano's destructive powers. Sadly, the town's residents – and curious onlookers – watched helplessly as the lava burned homes and buried most of the village. One of the famous sites from the town was an old stop sign, whose red warning still peeked out over a four-foot thick lava flow that covered the road and hardened around the sign. The family agreed that they would visit this town after seeing the volcano, the famous crater, and the lava flow at the Pu'u O'o vent.

After passing the prison chain gang, it took the Sanders family another half-hour to get into the park. "This darn traffic!" murmured Mr. Sanders more than once. Everyone in the car was getting restless to get out of the car and explore the volcano. So, as soon as they entered the park Mrs. Sanders had an idea.

"I know!" exclaimed Mrs. Sanders, pointing excitedly out the window. "Right there is the entrance to the Thurston Lava Tube. Why don't we go there first, then to the Halemau... er, the crater. Whatever it is called. You know, the famous crater where Madam Pele lives. Then we can see..."

Mrs. Sanders wasn't able to finish her sentence. A low grumbling sound rolled across the road. Each person in the large jeep felt it deep inside his or her stomachs. It came from directly beneath the road and seemed as if the Earth was waking up from a long slumber. It lasted several seconds.

"Whoa!" Isaac's eyes were wide and he was leaning forward. From his seat in the back, his head jutted between his parents in the front seat of the vehicle. "Wow! What was that?"

It was a few seconds before his father answered and when he did, his reply was more of a question than an answer. "The volcano," he said flatly, looking at Mrs. Sanders, who met his concerned gaze. Mrs. Sanders simply shrugged her shoulders. Neither of them had ever experienced an earthquake before.

"So that is what Madam Pele sounds like!" Said Isaac, "She should have eaten breakfast. Her stomach is rumbling."

But no one laughed at Isaac's joke. From their seat in the far back, the girls reached out to hold each other's hands. Mr. Sanders stopped the jeep. After several moments of silence, a grinning Isaac broke the spell. "This is going to be an exciting day," he was still smiling.

And that quickly, the sound was gone.

Spike seemed not to notice the excitement. Again. He still had his headset on and was obviously enjoying the music. His eyes were closed. His thin neck bee-bopped like a chicken to and fro to the sound inside his headset. Isaac looked sideways at Spike, noticed that his friend was oblivious of what the rest of them had just experienced, and decided not even to bother to tell him. From his vantage point in the driver's seat peering into the rearview mirror, Mr. Sanders smiled as he observed Isaac frown in disgust at Spike's disinterest.

It was Mr. Sanders who spoke next. After stopping the jeep when the rumbling swept across the volcano, he took off his glasses to clean them and commented, "Yeah, good plan." It was a belated response to his wife's recommendation to stop at the lava tube first. "The sign indicated the lava tube was close by," said Mr. Sanders, as if to reassure himself. "There should be a park ranger or tourists there. We can ask them about that rumbling sound."

The jeep continued down the road to the site. "There it is," the girls said in unison. Rebecca's head nodded to the side of the road where a sign pointed tourists to a parking lot near the lava tube. Surprisingly, there weren't many cars in the lot.

~~~

"What's a lava tube, Grandpa?" asked Andrew.

Andrew's question coincided with the high-pitched beep of the microwave oven. Grandpa's hot tea was ready downstairs in the kitchen. Putting the book down on his lap and clapping his hands on his knees, the old man said, "Let's go get my tea and I'll tell you."

Andrew climbed out of bed and joined his grandfather. He had just nestled into bed for the second night of the story, asking his mother if he could go to bed an hour early tonight in order to have extra time for the book.

"Well, the lava from Kilauea and Mauna Loa has been erupting for a very long time, Andrew. It poured through underground veins hundreds and even thousands of years ago. When the eruptions stopped, they left huge caves that look like long, eerie hallways under the ground. They are round like a big straw. Some stretch for a mile. The Thurston Lava Tube is a few hundred feet long and about as high as your bedroom ceiling."

They reached the kitchen and Andrew's grandfather prepared his tea. Before heading back upstairs he reached up into the top shelf of the pantry and took from a Tupperware container two cookies. As they climbed back up the stairs, Andrew's mother, who was watching television in the living room with her husband, spoke up. "No cookies for Andrew, Dad. It's nearly his bedtime." Andrew was always amazed at how his mother seemed to have eyes in the back of her head. She never even turned around to look at them or the kitchen.

"'Course it is." The old man winked at Andrew as he handed one of the cookies to the boy.

"So," he continued as they entered Andrew's bedroom, "there is no lava in the tube but it is filled with ancient lava and the old cave used to lead down to the main magma chamber!"

"Wow," muttered Andrew as he pulled the covers over his legs. "Cool," he said, nodding his head in agreement.

"Yeah, cool," smiled his grandfather.

~~~

"Here we are!" Exclaimed Isaac. "Let's go!"

Isaac, his sister, and Grace ran ahead. Isaac and his sister always wanted to be the first to do things – the first in line for rides at amusement parks, the first to walk through the door at the mall, the first to jump in the comfortable chair in the living room. But, given Rebecca's frightening accident, Isaac patiently took her hand, exchanged a knowing glance with his parents, and only then headed across the empty parking lot. But, once they passed the parking lot, the three kids raced toward the entrance of the lava tube. Spike was slower getting out of the big jeep but the excitement of the volcano seemed finally to be getting to him too because he ran to catch up with the others.

While much of the Hawaii Volcanoes National Park was barren fields of ancient, black lava, the area around the Thurston Lava Tube was a lush rainforest. A pathway winded through a forest of giant fern trees, resembling a scene from a fairy tale story. The ferns stretched overhead like opened umbrellas and the sunlight came through the cover only in streaks. The entrance to the lava tube was at the end of the snaking trail. The four kids ran along the path, stopping periodically to read the informational signs and listen to and look for the small, tropical birds that lived there. This gave the parents some long overdue time to talk in private.

As he was locking the vehicle, Mr. Sanders was the first to bring up the topic of Spike. He expressed his frustration with the boy and concern that Isaac would be influenced by him. By this time in the vacation, Mrs. Sanders had all but stopped defending Spike, no longer mentioning that his mother worked long hours and evenings, and that the boy's father had long ago abandoned the family. When Isaac had first started playing with Spike after school, the Sanders had asked other neighbors and parents from the school about Spike's family. They learned that no one knew when the boy's father had left. Obviously, it had been some time ago. Spike was often alone after school and in the evenings, and had to take care of himself. His older brother was of no help and a few neighbors suggested that it was the older brother who was the real troublemaker.

They also learned that none of their neighbors or the

parents of the children in Isaac's class knew Spike's mother. In fact, no one had even seen her at the parent-teacher meetings at school or at any of the school events. Spike, it seemed, walked to and from school by himself (technically, he skateboarded the short distance between his home and the school). Spike's mother's name was Sarah and she was a waitress at a small restaurant near the interstate highway outside of town. She worked long hours and the dinner shift.

Despite feeling sorry for Spike, Mrs. Sanders shared her husband's concern that Spike was not a good influence on Isaac and that Isaac seemed to be holding back from doing much of what he wanted to do in Hawaii because of his spiky-haired friend. Mrs. Sanders told her husband that she had called Spike's mother, as she had promised to do, four times since they arrived in Hawaii. But she ended up leaving messages every time. Each message was the same: Spike was well and everyone was having fun. Spike's mother had returned only one call, leaving a short message with the hotel's front desk. When Clara Sanders called back no one answered on the other line.

Both the Sanders hushed their conversation when a middle-aged Japanese couple and their young daughter walked by them on the pathway to the lava tube. The man smiled shyly and discreetly as they continued past John and Clara, who were hunched over a sign with pictures of the endangered birds on the island. They resumed their quiet conversation about Spike. Mr. Sanders pointed out that he thought Isaac was getting tired of Spike, and told his wife what he saw in the vehicle earlier when they felt the ground rumble beneath them.

"Mom, Dad! Hurry up!" It was Rebecca. The four kids were standing at the entrance of the lava tube waving their arms in the air.

"Coming!" Both John and Clara Sanders yelled at the same time. The rest of the conversation would have to wait until later. They were, however, delighted that Rebecca was enjoying herself. Sometimes the parents could hardly believe their daughter's remarkable recovery. Husband and wife looked thoughtfully at one another. They were both thinking the same thing: how their daughter had done so much better than the physicians had predicted. "Knock on wood," smiled Mrs. Sanders and tapped her fist on her husband's forehead. He only laughed.

~~~

Wet vegetation dangled from the top of the entrance of the lava tube, out of reach of Isaac's outstretched arm. It even had the smell of a greenhouse – damp and overpowering but somehow sweet. Huge arms of fern trees lurched over them. Everything was dark and slimy. Grace said that the entrance of the lava tube looked like the mouth of a giant serpent that had come up out of the earth. Isaac agreed. The rocks on the side even reminded him of old, rotted teeth.

Grace cupped her hands and yelled into the serpent's mouth: "H-e-l-l-o!" Smiling, Grace added an echo to her voice for effect. She jumped back momentarily, when a real voice responded "H-e-l-l-o!" It was the young Japanese girl that had entered the lava tube only a minute before them. All four of the kids let out a nervous giggle.

"Go on," said Spike sarcastically. "C'mon, you're not a chicken are you?" And Spike started clucking while walking around the entrance, popping his head to-and-fro like a chicken. Isaac laughed, thinking that Spike actually did look like a chicken.

"I'm not scared," answered Isaac, still smiling. "This place is awesome. Let's go!" He forgot his parents' request to wait for them at the entrance to the lava tube.

Isaac entered the snake's mouth, which darkened immediately once inside. Grace followed, then Rebecca, and finally Spike, who still had his headphones on. Heavy, black rocks lined both sides of the long, hollow tube. Years of moisture, which slowly trickled down from the ceiling, forming traces of little puddles throughout the walkway, had worn the walls smooth. They felt like wet glass. The exit was not visible and the slight curves and twists in the tunnel gave the appearance that it stretched forever. Small, yellowed lights jutted out every several feet in order to keep the inside of the lava tube lit. Barely. Wherever a light was found, small mosses and other wet plants clung to the walls of the cave near it, fed by the dull rays of the old lights. The whole scene gave the lava tube a mysterious and foreboding feel. The kids half expected a demon to jump out at them from around every twist and turn.

As the four kids walked through the lava tube their footsteps echoed down the tunnel like shots of a snare drum being hit. Periodic giggles from the two girls also filled the air and disrupted Isaac's thoughts of what it must have been like, thousands of years earlier, when molten hot lava poured through the very spot where he stood.

"Hey!" It was Mrs. Sanders. But she was too late, the kids had already entered the lava tube and the sound outside did not penetrate the long, underground corridor. Both husband and wife picked up their pace a little in order to catch up with the kids.

Suddenly, a soft rumble rolled over the ground beneath them. From the entrance of the lava tube, Mr. and Mrs. Sanders felt it. Deep inside the tube, Isaac reached out and braced himself against the cool, hard rock of the lava tube's wall. It felt as if he was on a fun-house ride at the carnival. He felt the shaking under his feet and momentarily lost his balance.

Rebecca called out nervously for her older brother. As she said his name, he heard her voice tremble. Isaac instantly reached out for her hand and assured her that everything was alright.

Just then, the lights mounted on the walls of the lava tube that lit the path through the underground chamber flickered. Rebecca repeated her brother's name. This time, Isaac felt

Grace grab his other hand. As the lights flickered again, they cast elongated and distorted shadows across the walls of the lava tube. The shadows of the four kids grew then shrunk before them with each flicker of the lights, as if performing a haunted dance.

"Hold still," Isaac tried to calm his sister and Grace. Over his shoulder he called out quietly, trying to calm his voice so as to not alarm the girls. "Mom. Dad. We're here." He shook his head from side to side, thinking how foolish his words sounded. Obviously, there was no response. He thought his parents were still outside the entrance to the lava tube. "Well," he looked at Rebecca and then Grace, "I mean, let's go back and meet them."

"Scared?" It was Spike.

"Nooo." Isaac's voice gave away his real feelings. He was worried. "I just think we ought to …"

At that moment, the kids heard Mr. Sanders call out their names. He started to tell them to stand still, that he was coming to get them. But, as he spoke a horrible, roaring sound came from every direction. The sound hurt Isaac's ears and was unlike anything he had ever heard before. It was lower and more powerful sounding than anything imaginable and it felt as if loud speakers were inside the lava tube blaring out the sound of an explosion. The pressure from the sound pounded in his head and nearly knocked all four kids off their feet.

Then rocks from the ceiling began to fall around them.

Small ones at first. Isaac froze in his tracks. His feet seemed to weigh a hundred pounds and were glued to the pathway. He was unable to take his eyes off the ceiling, but he was squeezing his sister's hand and Grace's hand. He thought to himself, "Mustn't let go. Mustn't let go of the girls."

Then the floor of the lava tube buckled beneath them. The entire lava tube shifted to the left. The earth was no longer firm and the force knocked all four children off their feet. Isaac fell awkwardly on his back, still holding onto the girls' hands, who fell with him. Rebecca landed on top of him. He saw her face in front of him. She was screaming but he could not hear her. The only sound was the explosion of earth and rock. Out of the corner of his eye Isaac saw Spike's arms flailing. He seemed to be launched into the air, flying away from them like a panicked bird. The roar was deafening and was now mixed with the very frightening sound of rocks cracking and the lava tube creaking.

Near the entrance of the lava tube, Mr. Sanders was in a full sprint to the kids when the impact occurred. It knocked him completely off his feet. Careening to his right, his outstretched leg and foot found no solid ground as they came down. He was hurled head-first into the wall, striking it at an odd angle. Lying on his stomach, Mr. Sanders felt himself losing consciousness.

A huge portion of the wall behind the kids collapsed, raining debris and lava rock across the walkway of the tunnel. From his back, Isaac looked up and over his shoulder to see the falling wall behind him. The impact of the wall crashing to the ground shook all four kids then lifted them up into the air again. As they fell back to earth, dust mushroomed up from the floor of the lava tube and enveloped Isaac and the two girls, blurring everything.

And then the entire ceiling gave way.

Chapter 7

Buried

"They're okay, right, Grandpa? I mean...," Andrew continued, "Isaac is alright, right?"

"Of course not. They just experienced a 7.2 earthquake." Andrew's grandfather then cleared his throat, swallowed, and said flatly, "It was a terrible quake. Terrible."

"I think it would be cool," answered Andrew.

His grandfather did not respond. Andrew caught the serious look and stopped talking.

~~~

The thin, faint beam of the flashlight pierced the darkness of the lava tube. The images of the children appeared ghostly in the dust that filled the air. The earthquake had knocked out the lights that used to brighten the pathway through the long lava tube. Now it was pitch black, except for the flashlight beam. Isaac experienced a new kind of darkness. Nighttime was one thing. But the absence of light below the earth was a different kind of blackness.

"You okay?" Isaac pointed the beam at Rebecca's face, which was next to his.

"Ah!" The bright, close light hurt her eyes. "I was until you blinded me," she complained.

"Good, you're the same, old Rebecca." His familiar teasing and smile calmed her. Inside, however, Isaac was worried sick. He remembered what it felt like when Rebecca was in the hospital. During her long recovery in the hospital and then back at home, he had vowed he would never let anything bad happen to her again. What would his parents think if… His panicked thoughts were interrupted.

"Over here." It was Grace. The voice sounded near and to Isaac's right. Fortunately, he had packed a flashlight in his backpack. Isaac always liked to be prepared. This time it paid off.

Grace repeated herself. She sounded remarkably calm. The beam from Isaac's flashlight first pointed directly up to the ceiling, then ran downward until both he and Rebecca saw Grace's face illuminated amidst the dust. She had a little blood on her lips but was alright.

"Grace!" Rebecca called out in a sighing voice, quiet but also excited to see her friend.

Isaac told Grace not to try standing. They all needed to be careful, he explained. Rocks were strewn everywhere and, every few minutes, a small piece of what used to be the ceiling of the lava tube fell to the ground. Grace nodded that she understood and very carefully Isaac and Rebecca stood and tried to dust the debris and dirt off their faces and out of their mouths.

After helping Grace up with his free hand, Isaac handed her the flashlight and told her to hold it steady. He then took a small water bottle out of his backpack and they each took a small sip – Isaac allowed only a little water – to wash the dust out of their mouths. He then called out for Spike. The sound echoed eerily down the lava tube. There was no answer, but they heard the shuffling of feet across the rocks. Grace pointed the flashlight in the direction of the sound and it revealed Spike's high-top sneakers rubbing back and forth on the ground. He was sitting with his arms hugging his bent knees, feet pushing the stones and debris around in front of him.

"You're alright." Isaac and Grace spoke in unison. The sound of their voices did not seem to awake Spike from his trance, but slowly he raised his head and stared blankly at them. The three kids walked, hand in hand, to Spike and Isaac grabbed Spike by the arm to help him stand. He was uninjured. Isaac offered Spike a sip of water but he did not respond to the gesture.

It was Isaac who took control of the situation. "Thank goodness we're all okay. Let's get back to the entrance of the lava tube to find mom and dad. Come on."

Isaac turned and started back from where they came. He walked no more than twenty feet, however, before coming to a wall of fallen rock. The collapsed ceiling of the lava tube formed a pile of boulders and mid-sized rocks stretching from one side of the cave to the other, and up ten feet to where the ceiling had once been.

"Isaac." It was Rebecca. She said his name as if it were a question. In an act of futility, Isaac walked up to the wall of rock, and pushed against one of the boulders roughly twice his own size. It did not budge. He pushed again.

"Can we climb over it?" asked Grace. "I mean, we've got to, right?"

"Hold this." Isaac handed Grace the flashlight and slowly started climbing the rocks, careful to press against each one to make sure it did not tumble down with him on it. Grace guided the beam of light in the direction of Isaac's hands as he very slowly crawled up two large boulders. Stretching his hand overhead, Isaac reached up to where the ceiling once stood. The beam of light showed only more rocks, extending up into what used to be the roof of the lava tube.

"Mom! Dad! Can you hear me?" Isaac shouted in the direction of the rock wall, which absorbed the sound. His voice sounded muffled and weak in the darkness and dense rock barrier. Rebecca joined in, shouting for a full two minutes before she started to weep.

There was no reply.

Isaac turned and said that it looked like they weren't

going to be able to climb across it. Silhouetted in the light, his face showed the dejection he felt. As Isaac started to explain that they should probably try to go out the exit of the lava tube and then circle back to look for his parents, the rock under his outstretched left foot gave way with a sharp groaning sound. It rolled away from the wall, causing Isaac to fall backward.

The girls screamed as he landed heavily on his back before them. His head hit hard and he was temporarily awash in a sharp pain. After a few minutes, he was able to shake off the grogginess. Rebecca and Grace knelt beside him. Rebecca was crying; Grace was shining the light too closely to his eyes. His hand pushed the beam away.

Both girls forgot that Isaac hated to be hugged. Isaac did too, as they hugged him tightly.

"Okay, okay." He waved them off. His head hurt and the pain shot through his neck and arms as he stood straight.

A moment later they realized Spike was not there. While they called out his name, Isaac took the flashlight and swept it in an arc, from right to left around the lava tube. In unison, they all called his name.

With Issac holding Rebecca's hand and Rebecca holding Grace's hand, the three started walking cautiously in the direction of the exit. Every few steps one of them called out for Spike. Rebecca's footing gave way once, while slipping off a loose rock, but both Isaac and Grace tightened their grip on her and she did not fall.

And there ahead of them, Isaac's flashlight caught the skull emblem shining on the black T-shirt. Spike stood there with a perplexed look on his face. Another wall of collapsed rock blocked his path.

"Spike?" Isaac's voice was stern and short. He did not need to say anymore. It was clear that he was upset that his friend had walked away from the group. Grace finished Isaac's thought: "We've got to stay together, Spike!"

A minute later, the beam of Isaac's flashlight revealed that it was possible to crawl around the right side of the rock wall. Only one boulder, roughly three feet high, rested against the far wall. Above it was an opening that led down the long, curved walkway of the lava tube. On account of all the dust kicked up by the earthquake, the faint beam of light only traveled about forty feet down the tube. But it revealed that there was nothing obstructing the way.

One by one, the four kids crawled over the boulder against the wall. Isaac pointed the light down at the boulder and offered an open hand to assist everyone over the rock.

As Spike stepped down off the boulder, the last to pass the obstacle, a slight voice echoed from the direction of the exit.

"Hey!" Rebecca called out. Isaac followed, calling out, "Is someone there? Can you hear me?"

"Shhh." Grace waved her hand at both of them.

There in the distance they heard voices. There were people down there and they understood one of the words to be "yes."

"We're coming!" The kids sang out in unison. Isaac pointed his flashlight across the walkway out in front of them, the beam searching for the person or persons in the distance. In their rush to get to the sound, however, Rebecca lost her footing and fell hard on her knee. Both Grace and Isaac reached out for her. Rebecca wanted to cry, but didn't, although tears welled up in the corner of her eyes. The thin beam of Isaac's flashlight revealed a small gash in her knee. Blood began to trickle out both sides of the gash.

"It's okay, Rebecca. I have something in my pack." Putting the flashlight in his mouth and gripping it with his teeth, Isaac unzipped the backpack and began pulling items from it. A bottle of water and a small thermos. A Swiss army knife with a bright, white cross on the red handle. A notebook. Granola bars from the hotel breakfast. The sight of them reminded Isaac of their predicament. Although they departed the hotel only a few hours earlier, it now seemed to him as if it were days ago. Finally, a small, yellow plastic container. Isaac's smile reassured Rebecca. He opened it to reveal a little first-aid kit he had purchased from the hotel gift shop when they arrived. Grace thought to herself that only Isaac would prepare such a backpack. But she was glad he did.

With water and gauze, Isaac cleaned Rebecca's wound and put all three Band-Aids the kit contained on her knee. The procedure completed, Grace squeezed her friend with a big hug. Rebecca's lips quivered, but she did not cry.

"Who was it that they heard in the tube?" Andrew asked his grandfather. "Was it Isaac's mother and father?"

"No," he answered. "Remember that they were back at the entrance of the lava tube. The voices came from the other direction."

Andrew protested, "But, maybe they had run around and came in from the other direction." His expression was hopeful, as if the power of suggestion could change the events in the story.

"No, afraid not," said the old man. "It turns out that it was actually..."

"The Japanese man. I mean, the man and his family." Andrew interrupted his grandfather, obviously pleased with the fact that he figured out the story, even though he still wanted it to be Isaac's parents. "The man and his family that passed them when they were about to go into the tube!"

"Yes, the same. Turns out his name was Okinaka. Now, let me continue..."

~~~

When the four kids rounded the next turn in the lava tube, a bend in the walkway to the left, they saw a young girl waving her hand over her face, as if to shield her eyes from the glare of the flashlight.

"Hello," a middle-aged woman knelt on one knee behind the girl. Isaac pointed the flashlight in her direction. She was a petite woman, not much taller than a young girl. Her hand rested on a man who was on the ground, propped up on his elbows but obviously in pain. His face grimaced with discomfort.

"Hi," Isaac responded.

"We heard you." Grace smiled. "We were back there." She pointed behind herself.

The woman continued. "Are you alone? Is there anyone else with you?" Her accent revealed that she was Japanese, but her English was rather proficient, despite the panic in her voice.

"Yes. I mean, no." Isaac shook his head. "I meant to say that my parents are back there but there is a huge pile of rocks that blocked our way back out. They fell from the ceiling during the earthquake."

"We're gonna go this way and find them," said Rebecca. She pointed toward the exit, still a few hundred feet away.

"Is he hurt?" Grace was looking at the man lying on his side.

"He is my husband. Yoshi." The woman answered. She introduced herself as Masume and her young daughter as Keiko. The Okinakas were from Japan. Everyone smiled nervously, not knowing what to say; everyone that is but Spike, who stared absently off into the blackness of the cave. Isaac wanted to hurry everyone along and escape the lava tube.

Masume Okinaka quickly told the children that a boulder landed on her husband's leg and broke it. She also apologized that he didn't speak English. Mr. Okinaka understood however that his wife was talking about him, and he managed through clenched teeth to say "hello." But he did not smile. Their daughter looked as if she was about to cry until Grace reached out and touched her hand, calming the young girl. As Grace gently squeezed Keiko's hand she told her how old she was. Rebecca did the same. It worked. Keiko whispered back her own answer and the girls formed an instant bond. The meeting also had the effect of making Rebecca forget the pain in her knee.

This was the Okinaka family's third visit to Hawaii, the first while Yoshi Okinaka was on business. A representative from an investment firm, Mr. Okinaka was often in Hawaii on business. His company owned several luxury resorts in Honolulu. He had planned a family vacation but urgent business presented itself so the trip turned out to be a working vacation for Yoshi. He concluded two days of meetings, filed his report to his superiors, and had arrived on the Big Island yesterday for the express purpose of taking his wife and daughter to the volcano.

Isaac offered each of them water, opening a new bottle from his backpack. He had three small bottles and his thermos. The Okinakas were all grateful. Mr. Okinaka said something in a serious voice to his wife, who translated. They wanted to know if the four kids knew how to get out of the lava tube. Isaac nodded in agreement and said that he thought they ought to get moving. The Okinakas looked at one another for a long moment, then Mrs. Okinaka said in a solemn voice that her husband was unable to walk.

No one answered her and Isaac tried to think of something encouraging to say, knowing that he wanted to leave the lava tube and find his parents right away. The silence, however, was broken by a powerful rumble.

Another earthquake!

The ground again rolled mightily, as if the floor was pulled out from under them. The earth roared and the rocks around them groaned as they were squeezed and then loosened from the walls. "Not again," Isaac thought to himself. "This can't be happening again."

Rebecca's scream was cut off by Grace who yelled, "Cover your heads!"

Everyone did as they were told as a large boulder crashed directly behind Rebecca and Grace. The impact sounded like a bomb went off and Rebecca spun around and lurched away from the crash. But she lost her balance and seemed to float in the air for a moment. Isaac was powerless to help her, as he had been knocked off his feet and fell forward hard against the floor. His flashlight streamed rays of light across the ceiling as it flew from his hand. In the spiraling light he managed to see his sister land heavily on her side. Her arm bent backward in an awkward angle.

Rebecca's shriek rang out amid the crashing explosions of

the rocks. Yoshi Okinaka also screamed out in pain when his wife was knocked off balance and landed on his broken leg.

All around them rocks of varying sizes cascaded to the ground. Isaac was sure he would be crushed like a bug under a boot. He squeezed his hands tightly over his head and, instinctively, curled into a ball. But, all the while his eyes darted for a sign of his sister. It was no use. The flashlight hit the ground not far from him and the light went black.

The sound of the rocks and earth groaning were amplified in the total darkness that enveloped them. This quake lasted much longer than the one before it. It was nearly a minute before the destruction fell silent.

Chapter 8

Daylight

Isaac was the first to speak. "Rebecca, where are you?" He could hear her crying, but in the confusion and blackness he had trouble orienting himself. The sensation was strange – in the pitch black and thick dust he could not tell up from down or left from right.

"Over here!" called out Grace. She was no more than two feet from Isaac but in the dusty, dark cave he could not see her. In fact, he could not have seen her even if she was waving her hands in front of his face.

"Are you alright?" Isaac asked. "Give me your hand." Isaac moved his hand slowly in an arc in front of his body and, after a few tries, felt Grace's outstretched hand. "Grace," he said in a quiet voice. He felt her hand squeeze his hand tightly. Curiously, Isaac felt a sense of calm wash over him. There was comfort knowing he was not alone. He was exhausted but was not panicked. "Calm," he reminded himself. "Stay calm. Stay in control."

Isaac heard the Okinakas calling out for their daughter, Keiko. They were speaking in Japanese and the girl called out in a quiet voice. Isaac could hear the fear in her wavering voice.

Suddenly, the piercing beam of the flashlight shot upward through the dust-filled cave. Grace had found the flashlight with her free hand. It had been lying on the ground next to her. Everyone let out a sigh of relief and Grace handed the flashlight to Isaac, who pointed it first in the direction of his sister. Slowly, the beam of light traveled across the debris-strewn floor of the lava tube and, after a few seconds, came to rest on Rebecca's body. She was sobbing and lying on her side about ten feet from Isaac and Grace. She was holding her arm, clutching it against her chest.

In the quake, Rebecca had been knocked violently to the ground and had broken her right wrist. Isaac stood and walked toward Rebecca, talking reassuringly to her as he navigated the rocks and cracks in the floor. Grace followed him. As Isaac was saying his sister's name, his foot slipped on the side of an angled rock on the floor and he fell sharply to the ground, slicing open his right knee. The pain shot through his body but he restrained the urge to yell out, instead clenching his teeth and holding his breath for what must have been a full minute before he slowly exhaled and let out a soft groan.

When he pointed the flashlight at his leg, he saw the

blood in the faded light and dust. It appeared like a dark ooze, circling an inch-long gash on the top of his knee. "Ohhh," muttered Grace as she looked over Isaac's shoulder at the cut. After assuring Grace he was alright, Isaac hobbled over to Rebecca.

As Isaac and Grace slowly turned Rebecca on her side, the young girl let out a scream. It was indeed her wrist. Grace shrieked a reminder to Isaac to be careful. Rebecca's eyes were as wide as saucers and were filled with pain. Isaac did not need to ask her if her wrist was broken. When he pointed the flashlight at his sister he saw that her wrist jutted out at an unnatural angle. "Oh, boy," he thought to himself. "This couldn't get much worse." But it was about to get a lot worse.

From over his shoulder, Isaac heard Mrs. Okinaka ask if everyone was okay. Isaac answered that they were alright and pointed the flashlight at the family. Keiko had found her way back to her parents' side. Yoshi Okinaka was rolling back and forth on his back, holding his leg. It was clear he was in a lot of pain.

Then Isaac remembered he had a second, smaller light in his backpack, so he asked Grace to unzip the backpack and take out the small pen-light he had packed. It did not provide much light, but every bit helped. As Grace helped Rebecca to sit up, Isaac called out for Spike. In the confusion of the second quake, the realization came to him that he had completely forgotten about Spike. On the third call, Spike answered. He said only one word: "Here."

Isaac and Mrs. Okinaka discussed their options. Isaac wanted to leave the lava tube immediately. It was not safe and he worried about another quake. Plus, Rebecca needed to see a physician and his parents were likely worried sick about the children. Mrs. Okinaka agreed and, after conferring with her husband in Japanese, he too nodded his head in the affirmative without saying anything. He was still clenching his teeth in pain. As they spoke, Isaac removed his short-sleeved, button shirt he wore over a T-shirt. He tore one of the sleeves off and wrapped it around his leg, tying a tight knot on the side of the knee away from his cut. Blood had trickled the entire way down his leg and into his shoe, but he hoped the shirt would help stop the bleeding.

Masume Okinaka told Isaac that her husband was unable to walk. With her eyes, she emphasized her comments in a way that would not frighten her young daughter, but she was clearly implying that her husband's leg was very badly broken. Isaac nodded back that he understood. As he turned and explained to Grace and Rebecca that they needed to leave now, he heard Mrs. Okinaka talking in a calm voice to her daughter. Although he could not understand what she was saying, he guessed correctly that Mrs. Okinaka wanted Keiko to leave with the other children. All the while, Yoshi Okinaka, who was now groggy from the pain of the severe break in his leg, protested under his breath. Isaac did not need to speak Japanese to know that Yoshi was telling his wife to leave him behind. But she refused to do so.

Tears welled up in Keiko's eyes as the five children walked away from the Okinakas. Isaac gave Mrs. Okinaka his pen-light and offered them a bottle of water, but Mr. Okinaka grunted in a way that made it clear he would not accept it. As they walked, Isaac used the rest of his torn shirt to make a crude sling for Rebecca's arm. He tied it around Rebecca's neck, allowing her arm to rest against her body, supported by the shirt-sling. She continued to clutch her wrist and, with each cautious step they took, she let out a soft groan. Rebecca was in a lot of pain.

Isaac was surprised at how quickly the light from the small pen-light had faded. The children had walked not more than 50 yards and they could no longer see any sign of the pen-light or the Okinakas. Grace seemed to be reading Isaac's mind and put her hand behind Keiko's head in a way that prevented her from turning around to look back into the blackness. Isaac had promised Mrs. Okinaka he would take care of Keiko and he intended to do it.

As the children walked over the rocks, Isaac pointed the flashlight down at their steps. Grace held Keiko's hand and Spike followed them without saying a word.

~~~

"You mean they left the Okinakas behind?" yelled young Andrew. "How could they do that? I mean, couldn't Mr. Okinaka walk at all?"

His grandfather answered flatly, "His leg was broken."

Andrew protested, not liking the answer he was given. "I mean, what happened to them? They got out of the lava tube, right?"

"Well, let's wait and see. First things first." The old man continued reading from the book.

~~~

Another hundred yards through the lava tube and the children came to a wall of boulders and rocks. As Isaac pointed the flashlight upward he saw that the ceiling had completely collapsed. They were trapped. Rocks behind; rocks in front. After telling Rebecca to stand still, he walked from one side to the other, peering into the rocks for a way through the enormous pile of hardened black lava.

Five minutes later he confirmed his worst fear. "We're stuck," he murmured. "No way through." Isaac shook his head in disappointment. "The entrance to the lava tube where we came from is also blocked." Dejected, he sat down on the rocks, his head lowered.

"Isaac!" It was Rebecca. "What are we going to do?" She called out as if doing so could change their predicament. Grace put her other arm around her friend. All three girls stood looking at Isaac. Isaac felt the weight of responsibility. He always did when it came to his sister, given what had happened to her on account of his actions. But now all three were looking to him for an answer. He was the older brother, but he did not know what to do.

Spike had been of no use. He had barely spoken since the first quake. Then, to Isaac's surprise, Spike spoke up.

"I think I saw a hole in the ceiling of the cave." Isaac's head snapped up to attention. His flashlight shined on Spike's face. It was covered in dust and sweat. Only part of his spiky hair remained standing. "Back behind us," Spike said. The tone of his voice was flat but Isaac detected a little hint of Spike's cockiness returning. The boy shrugged his head in the direction they had just come from. "Follow me," he said.

Isaac did. They all followed.

As Isaac trailed Spike through the dark tunnel he felt contradictory emotions. On the one hand, he felt embarrassed and somewhat defeated. He was trying to take care of his sister and the situation but it was Spike who spotted the hole in the ceiling and who everyone now followed...and did so naturally as if Spike was in charge, even though he had said virtually nothing since the first quake. Isaac felt like kicking himself for not seeing the hole and for not thinking of anything to say when Spike told the small party to follow him.

It was typical of Spike to be so hot and cold in his personality. This always frustrated Isaac and made him feel like he was trying too hard to be Spike's friend, while Spike, at times, seemed to barely notice Isaac. It had happened on more than one occasion in school when Isaac had called out to his "friend" in the hallways between classes, only to receive no gesture – not even a "hey" from Spike. When this happened, Isaac quickly withdrew his outstretched hand as if he had never waved to begin with and hoped that no one had seen the incident. At other times, Spike wanted to come to Isaac's house after school to "hang out."

The aloofness also happened just days before leaving for Hawaii, when Isaac's parents felt it was necessary to invite Spike to dinner at the Sanders' home in order to better get to know him. They had invited his mother too, but she could not get off work that day. Spike barely spoke during dinner and did not finish the meal Mrs. Sanders had so carefully prepared based on Isaac's suggestions of what Spike liked to eat. After dinner when Isaac announced proudly that he had an "awesome" video on Hawaii for the two of them to watch, Spike showed no interest. A few minutes into the show, during Isaac's favorite part of the video – a reenactment of the conquest and unification of the islands by Hawaii's first king, Kamehameha I – Isaac asked Spike what he thought about one of the bloodiest battles of the conflict. To Isaac's horror, Spike said simply, "Lame."

Isaac hoped his parents had not heard the comment but knew they had. That is when his mother stopped the video and suggested the boys ride bikes or Spike's skateboard. That worked. The two of them played outside for nearly one hour until, suddenly, Spike announced that he was tired and had to go home. The car ride back to Spike's house was an awkward one as no one in the car said a word, including Isaac's mother who was usually very chatty while driving.

Back in the lava tube, not far in the direction from where they had walked, Isaac spotted a faint ray of light peering through the ceiling. Dust kicked up from the earthquake wafted through the light, but it was clear that the light came from above. It was a way out!

"There," said Spike. "The flashlight." His voice was a demand, not a question. He held his hand out in the direction of Isaac. Isaac hesitated but then handed over the flashlight.

Spike began to climb up a pile of rocks, stumbling twice as he did. The others simply stood in the dark and watched him. After about ten minutes he reached the hole in the ceiling. In the light from the small hole, Isaac saw Spike turn his head and look down at the four of them standing at the base of the pile of boulders. Isaac yelled out, "Can you fit through the hole?"

Spike did not answer but began wriggling his body through the small opening. It looked like a very tight squeeze. So tight, in fact, that there was virtually no free room on either side of Spike as he squeezed his shoulders through the hole. When he did, it blocked out the light and the four children below stood in complete darkness.

"Spike!" Isaac called out a second time. "Wait, give me the flashlight!" But the soles of Spike's dirty sneakers were pulled up and through the hole. Isaac felt the pangs of panic starting. They had no flashlight. Grace joined Isaac in calling out Spike's name.

But then Spike's head peered down at them through the hole in the ceiling. "Here. Catch." And he lobbed the flashlight in Isaac's direction. The light was still on and its beam spun in circles around the cave as the flashlight flew through the air. Isaac felt his reflexes tighten. "Gotta catch it!" he thought to himself. And he did!

"Phew!" Isaac exhaled in relief, clenching the flashlight with both hands. Beside him he heard Grace also exhale in relief.

"Spike!" The kids all called out his name. There was no reply. He was gone.

~~~

"You mean he just left them behind?" Andrew was angry. "I knew he couldn't be trusted. I never liked him." Andrew's voice was firm.

"Well, I suppose I didn't either," said his grandfather.

Andrew continued, "You should never leave your friends. I never would! I hope Isaac kicks his butt when he finds him!"

"Now, Andrew," his grandfathered gave him that look, the same one his mother used when she was upset.

"Sorry, Grandpa."

"No need to apologize. I felt the same way," Grandpa admitted. And that quickly, the stern look was gone. With a playful wink, Grandpa continued the story.

~~~

"Come on, let's get out of here now." Isaac's voice was firm. He now regretted giving Spike the flashlight in the first place. "That is it," he thought to himself. "That is the last time I ever listen to him." Isaac felt guilty and embarrassed, as if his friends had turned to him to lead them from the lava tube and he could not even manage to stand up to Spike.

It took the four children about twenty minutes to climb the boulders. It was slow going. Rebecca could not use her arm and she was hesitant to take every step, the pain of her broken wrist was made worse with each bump and effort. Isaac patiently helped his sister, putting his hands around her hips to steady her. When he tried to pull her up from her underarms, Rebecca screamed out in pain. It was another five minutes before she would move. Isaac prompted her upward by reminding her, "Remember, 'Becca, there's nothing you can't handle!"

Keiko and Grace turned out to be skilled climbers, even better than Isaac. When they finally reached the hole it was a very tight squeeze. Keiko went first and climbed through the hole with ease. Isaac pushed her up from the bottom and, when he did, he nearly lost his balance on the loose boulders and fell off the pile of rocks. Grace's hand shot out to steady him. "Thanks," Isaac muttered. "Up you go." Grace was second. She was thin like Spike but, although younger, was already the same height.

Grace peered down through the hole, her open arms encouraging Rebecca to climb up. "It's safe up here. We're back on the ground," Grace explained. "I mean, you know, we're back on top of the lava tube on solid ground. There's trees…" She stopped her explanation. "Come on, Rebecca, you can do it. We'll find your parents."

And with that, Rebecca summoned the courage. She screamed out in pain as she pulled herself up with her good hand, with Isaac pushing from behind and Grace pulling her up by the arm.

Isaac followed.

Chapter 9

Mistake

The landscape around them had changed. The earth itself had shifted. A huge gash, like a giant cut, scraped across the ground before them and stretched as far as they could see. From an opening in the ground, scorching hot steam billowed up in soft but deadly plumes. The parking lot and entrance to the lava tube were nowhere in site.

The bright sky from that morning had already grown gray as clouds had drifted overhead during the brief time they were in the lava tube. Isaac now understood the weatherman's joke from the night before on the local television broadcast when he advised tourists not to worry about the threat of showers and cloudy skies because, "If you don't like the weather on the Big Island, wait thirty minutes and it will change."

A mist now covered the ground and hung in the air like the faint spray of a hose downwind. Everything seemed wet.

Despite the cloud cover, each of the four kids rubbed their eyes as they emerged from the darkness of the cave. Rebecca even asked Isaac if he had her sunglasses. He did not, although he usually carried more than enough supplies in his backpack. But what Isaac noticed most was the strong, pungent smell of sulfur. From every direction, the cracks in the ground spilled steam from an underground vent. It was a putrid smell. Not sharp and acidic like a skunk's spray, but just as repulsive.

Standing for a moment, still in disbelief at the events that had just transpired, Isaac was snapped out of his trance by Rebecca's shout. She was the first to yell out, "Mom! Dad!" No reply. A few seconds later Isaac joined his sister in calling out for their parents. The brother and sister exchanged a sideways glance, both looking nervous.

"Where's Spike?" questioned Grace. All four children scanned the terrain from side to side. Putting her hands on her hips in frustration, Grace added "He couldn't have just disappeared. He wouldn't have just left us, would he?"

"No." Isaac was not sure why he answered as he did, because he was thinking the opposite. Isaac called out his friend's name once. After about two minutes of silence he added, "Well, he was a good ten or twenty minutes or so ahead of us. Come on, everyone, the parking lot is over there. This sulfur smell is dangerous. We had better get out of here fast." He pointed off in the direction of a small knoll covered in fern trees. "Do you remember those trees when we first entered the lava tube?"

In unison, Rebecca and Grace nodded in agreement. "So, Mom and Dad will probably be over there," Rebecca smiled and seemed to finally perk up. She added, "Yeah, let's get out of here. This smell is, like, it is scaring me, Isaac."

"Me too," he admitted.

"It's creeping me out too," agreed Grace.

The pain from the broken wrist had really been bothering Rebecca and this was the first time since the ceiling of the lava tube collapsed that she held her head up. Impulsively she took two quick steps in the direction of the slight incline but pulled back in pain, with the sharp reminder from her wrist.

"Are you okay?" asked Grace.

"It hurts. Bad." Rebecca's voice was again subdued.

Isaac put his arm around Rebecca. "Come on, we'll all go together." And the four children walked cautiously up the crested hill for about one hundred yards until they were atop it. From their vantage point, the scene was eerie. The gash in the ground was twice the size in the parking lot, so large that it had nearly swallowed up one of the cars. The back two tires were sunk down into the hole, giving the car the appearance of being alive and trying to cling with its front two tires to the ledge of the gash.

There was no sign of anyone. Just three vacant cars, including the one being swallowed whole by Madam Pele. Isaac could not contain himself any longer and he ran down the hill in advance of the three girls, shouting his parents' names. There was no reply. No answer from anyone. When he arrived at the entrance to the Thurston Lava Tube he saw that the staircase leading down to the trail had collapsed. There was an awkward gap of several feet between the railing and the slabs of concrete and debris strewn about below them. The large sign at the entrance to the lava tube was now bent curiously over the missing staircase like an awning angled to provide shade.

Isaac continued calling his parents' names. Grace, Rebecca, and Keiko finally caught up with him. All four now stood looking down at the walkway to the entrance of the lava tube.

"I can make it down there," said Isaac. "You three stay here. Better yet, go to the jeep and see if it is open. You can wait in dad's rented jeep. Close the windows. Maybe it will keep the sulfur smell out."

"Isaac..." Rebecca's voice sounded worried.

"Go with Grace. You'll be alright." Isaac looked up at Grace, who understood and took Rebecca by the hand. "No," complained Rebecca. "I mean you be careful!"

"Yeah, Isaac, don't go back in the lava tube. It isn't safe and the..." Grace's voice trailed off without completing her sentence. She didn't want to mention the earthquake. None of them did. The girls waited long enough to see Isaac climb part way down the collapsed staircase, then jump – in a way that was more of a fall – the remainder of the way to the walkway. He landed hard but managed to catch his balance without ending up on the ground.

"I'm okay," he murmured. "Go to the jeep."

Isaac walked the short way through the large fern trees and pathway snaking in an "S" formation to the entrance of the lava tube. He thought it odd that not a single fern tree had fallen. They looked exactly as they had when he first passed by them on his way to the entrance of the lava tube a half hour ago. It was as if there had not been an earthquake. But there was no sound from the birds that inhabited the fern forest. The thought sent a shiver up his back and he ran the rest of the way down the trail to the entrance.

Then his heart dropped when he arrived. What had been a large opening into the cave was now a scene of destruction. Rocks and boulders of all sizes were littered across the ground. The lush vines and plants that decorated the sides of the opening were no longer there. Just rocks. The hill above the opening had obviously collapsed, and wet mud cascaded across the rocks at a forty-five degree angle.

Isaac stood with his toes touching the edge of the mud and rocks. It was obvious to him that there was no way to get back into the lava tube. His mind raced with fantastical ideas. He was angry with himself for thinking of such crazy ideas as running to get a bulldozer to clear away the rocks and mud. But where would he find a bulldozer? He even thought about going back to the small crevice through which they had managed to escape from the lava tube. No, that too was ridiculous! He had to find his parents and get help for the Okinakas.

Plus, what if there was another quake?

The thought snapped him out of his absurd ideas and he yelled again, "Mom, Dad. Are you in there? Can you hear me?" He repeated himself four or five times. His voice seemed weak, weaker than he had ever realized. "Were they in there and could they hear him?" he thought to himself.

"Isaac!" It was Grace. He could not see her because of the canopy of fern trees above and all around him. But, he could make out her voice. The direction of her voice told him she was standing at the collapsed stairway.

"I'm here!" he answered.

"Come back!" Grace yelled.

Isaac's initial response was that something must be wrong. Something must have happened to Rebecca! His moment of panic lessened when he realized the tone of Grace's voice did not sound alarmed. "Coming!" he responded. "Be there in a minute." He turned and ran back up the trail.

All three girls were standing, looking down at him. Isaac was glad to see them – make that thrilled to see them. It had only been five minutes, but being alone brought out anxieties and Isaac made a mental note that the four of them were better off sticking together from then on. They would not separate.

It took Isaac several tries to climb back up the muddy wall that had once contained a staircase. His feet kept slipping and there was nothing to grip. He had not thought of climbing back up when he slid and jumped down. "The jeep?" he questioned, his chest weaving from the exertion of trying to climb the sheer muddy wall.

"It was locked," Rebecca blurted out. As Isaac was about to ask if they had seen Mom and Dad, Rebecca finished his thought, saying "They weren't there. Isaac, I don't know where they are." Rebecca started to cry.

~~~

Andrew suppressed his concern about the children's predicament. In a calm voice, he told his grandfather: "Isaac's parents must be stuck in the lava tube. How could they have made it out? The earthquake must have buried them."

He did not ask any more questions, as if he did not want to hear the answer. This time his grandfather let him talk without saying a word. Andrew continued his assessment of the situation, offering his guess on the whereabouts of Spike and whether the Okinakas would survive another earthquake.

"They should go back to the jeep. Maybe the keys are in it or … I mean, they could break the window open. I don't know Grandpa." Andrew was rambling. Finally, he stopped and said, "Go ahead, keep reading." And his grandfather did.

~~~

Squeezing Rebecca's hand, Grace asked Isaac, "Did you see anything in the lava tube?" Isaac explained what he had encountered. He left out the other thoughts that began slipping into his mind. He shook the thoughts free and wiped the sweat and hair from his eyes. Isaac then turned his attention to the wall of rock and mud, studying it and realizing he needed to start being more careful and thoughtful. The gravity of their situation was dawning on him.

Isaac kicked and punched small dimples into the muddy wall, enough for his toes to get a grip. Pushing with his legs, Isaac managed to finally climb his way up to the parking lot.

As the children walked through the parking lot, they still did not see anyone. Isaac thought to himself that one of the three cars must have belonged to the Okinakas. So, who owned the third? The heaviness returned when he realized another person or family must be trapped inside the lava tube. Arriving back at the rented jeep, Isaac absently tried the door handle. It was locked. He then realized what he had done and looked at Grace as if to say, "Yes, you told me it was locked."

Isaac told the girls to find a rock. It did not take long. There were pieces of the macadam parking lot everywhere and the gaping hole in the ground that zigzagged across the parking lot contained lots of small rocks. Keiko spoke for the first time since they left her parents: "Here. I found a rock."

With two hands she held up a piece of what had been the parking lot, struggling to hold something the size of her head. Isaac thanked her then told everyone to stand clear. He slammed the macadam into the driver's side window, squinting his eyes.

Nothing happened. Nothing, except that the macadam broke into several smaller pieces. Isaac had not expected that. He thought the window would shatter.

Rebecca protested, reminding her brother that their father would be angry to find his window broken. Plus, the jeep was not theirs. Isaac did not answer, as he eyed a large rock back near where he had climbed up from the walkway to the entrance of the lava tube.

Returning with the rock, Isaac told everyone in a firm voice to move away. He cocked the rock behind him like a pitcher about to deliver a strike, and threw it at the window. It bounced back and struck him on the shoulder. The blow hurt and Isaac winced with pain and surprise, grasping his shoulder with his opposite hand. The window did not break, but there was a large crack in the shape of a spider web across the top of the window. Despite the pain in his shoulder, Isaac picked up the rock and immediately threw it again at the window. This time it worked.

A section of the window broke and the spider web grew in size. With the rock now inside the jeep, Isaac instructed the girls to get additional rocks. They did and three more throws from him succeeded in busting out the window.

Isaac removed his backpack and placed it on the jagged glass at the bottom of the window so he would not get cut, and pushed himself up and into the driver's seat, his backside and legs jutting out the door. Once inside he opened the door. Grace clapped and Rebecca smiled. She had disapproved of the whole venture but now celebrated their small accomplishment.

Isaac opened all the doors. Without having to be told, Grace climbed in and seemed to know what Isaac had in mind. Isaac told Rebecca and Keiko to stay outside. There was glass everywhere in the jeep. "Here," Isaac said flatly, handing Rebecca his backpack. Together, Isaac and Grace found another bottle of water. Warm but drinkable. They also found the park map they were given when they stopped at the Visitor Center, a large bag Mrs. Sanders had packed that contained a change of clothing for everyone, sunscreen, sunglasses, and two more granola bars. But they could not find the keys to the jeep.

The kids collected the items and stuffed them into Isaac's backpack. Grace carried the empty bag. Isaac opened the park map but they all had some trouble reading it. So Isaac decided to simply follow the road out of the entrance to the lava tube. However, when they rounded the curving road, they saw that the gash in the parking lot widened and cut across the entrance to the road. Rebecca protested, suggesting that they should all simply sit in the jeep. The four children stood for a moment pondering their next move.

"That way." Isaac spoke, pointing at a sign near the entrance. It had an arrow directing drivers to "The Chain of Craters Road." Isaac looked at the map and noticed there were several tourist sites marked along that road, including picnic grounds, rest stops, fields of ancient Hawaiian rock carvings known as petroglyphs, and the beach.

"There's bound to be people along this route," said Isaac. Grace agreed. "And we've got to get away from this sulfur and go get help." All four of them slowly set out, skirting the large hole in the road and heading downhill toward the water. As they walked they called out for Mr. and Mrs. Sanders, and even occasionally for Spike. The road was curiously undamaged. Isaac opened one of the granola bars, which they all shared, and then passed around the warm bottle of water. Warm water and mom's healthy snacks never tasted so good!

Little did they know they had made a mistake and were heading in the wrong direction.

Chapter 10

Wave

The four kids walked for about thirty minutes. The road was deserted and the sun beat off the macadam highway under their feet. It had the effect of draining everyone's energy. Plus, the stress of their ordeal in the collapsed lava tube caught up with the small party. Everyone was emotionally drained and still confused. The progress down the road was slow on account of Rebecca, whose fractured wrist ached with every step.

Two cars raced past them, heading up the hill toward the Visitor Center and out of the park. The first came around a corner with such speed that Isaac pushed the girls off the side of the road. All four of them rolled into the stones on the side of the two-lane road named Chain of Craters. The second car came nearly as fast but Isaac saw it and waved his arms frantically overhead in an effort to get the car to stop. A young couple sat in the front, their eyes wide with fear. They also did not stop; nor did they even slow down. Grace complained loudly at the cars' failure to offer help.

Isaac was surprised there weren't more cars. He reasoned that the others must have abandoned the National Park as soon as the earthquake struck. This made sense to him. But, Isaac was not thinking straight. It did not dawn on him that he should not be headed in the direction from which the cars were fleeing – which was the coastline farther down the slope of the volcano. Nor did he figure out that there may have been a reason the drivers, in their panic, did not stop to aid his small party.

"Isaac, I'm tired." It was Rebecca. She did not look good. She was afraid, worried, and exhausted. The crude sling he had fashioned for her using his shirt had slipped too far in the direction of her elbow and was hardly accomplishing its purpose.

"Let's stop," Isaac said. There was no complaint from anyone. The three girls sat down under a small tree on the side of the road, desperate to take advantage of the chance to get out from under the sun. Isaac sat beside them, keeping an eye on the road for the next passing car.

While Isaac fixed the shirt-sling, he thought to himself how much hotter it was at the volcano than at their resort, where there always seemed to be a refreshing breeze. Finally sitting down to relax, he became aware of how thirsty he was and re-moved another bottle of water from his backpack and passed it around. The girls drained its contents very quickly. As they did, Isaac arrived at a thought: perhaps all the ancient black lava that carpeted much of the volcano's mountainous slopes absorbed the heat from the sun and made it hotter. Plus, the volcanic activity below the surface must have super-heated the ground. He liked his new theory and made a mental note that *if* – no, make that *when* – they were safe and back home he would find out why it was so much hotter at the volcano.

"Where are we going?" Grace's question was not rude or doubting. In fact, she did not even look at Isaac when speaking. Her head hung low between her bent knees. Her T-shirt was covered in dirt from the lava tube and sweat.

Isaac was not sure how to answer but told his companions that there were some popular tourist sites listed on the map just ahead of them and that the ocean was just around the next bend. So, surely there had to be people there…and perhaps his parents. Moreover, the deep gash that crossed the landscape also happened to cut across the road leading back to the Visitor Center at the entrance of the National Park. It was therefore difficult to head back up the volcano toward the entrance. So, toward the ocean it was. Plus, it was easier to hike downhill than uphill…and it was away from the lava tube!

And then he felt it. At first it was but a very slight tremor under his feet. Isaac slowly looked over toward the girls, hoping they had not felt it. But they had. All three of them looked up and met his gaze. Keiko put her hands out to her sides as if to steady herself…and ready herself for what was about to come. For a full minute no one spoke. Or breathed. They just waited.

Nothing happened. "Thank goodness," thought Isaac. Though deliriously tired, Isaac wanted to get moving. He urged his friends to get back on their feet and get moving, reminding them that help was probably just around the next corner and that they would soon see the ocean below them. No one mentioned the tremor but everyone stood and started walking. Isaac was not sure why, but he felt better about walking. It made him feel like he was doing something, even if walking away from the lava tube really did not mean he was getting away from the volcano. The entire park was one huge volcano. At least the road on which they walked was downhill, very gradually declining from the heights of the park's entrance to sea level below.

"There!" Isaac was several feet in front of the others and was thus the first to spot the ocean. As they rounded a crest of craggy, black lava that had hardened hundreds of years ago into the shape of an eagle's head, Isaac saw a small strand of palm trees near the water's edge. It was a few hundred yards below them.

Most of the landscape between the kids and the ocean had long ago been stripped of any vegetation. Periodic lava flows over the past thousand years had given the surface of the sloping mountain the appearance of the surface of the moon or mars. It reminded him of the photos he had seen when visiting the planetarium on a recent school trip. Other than an occasional island of trees, the only sign of life was the road they were on that cut through the black fields of lava rock, winding in a meandering "S" from the spot they stood to what appeared to be a walkway far below.

Isaac removed his backpack and took out a compact case holding his binoculars. "There," he blurted out. "I see a walkway with a railing. Two wooden huts. They look a bit like the tiki huts at our hotel. A few palm trees…"

"But, do you see any people?" It was Rebecca.

"No, but it looks like the lava-viewing platform marked on the map," answered Isaac. The lava flow occasionally moved as new, underground lava tubes were created with each earthquake. Lava oozed slowly but deadly from the Pu'u O'o vent down to the Pacific Ocean a thousand feet below. The pictures in the Visitor Center showed a plume of smoke exploding up into the sky from where the molten hot lava met with the cool ocean waters. It was not far from the point Isaac was now peering at through his binoculars. He saw the wispy curl of smoke rising up from the lava pouring into the sea. And he saw something else.

"There are two cars," began Isaac.

"But where are the people?" It was Rebecca again. Isaac started to put down his binoculars to try and reassure his sister and Keiko, who looked like she was ready to cry. The small girl had been remarkably brave through this terrible day. But, as he lowered the binoculars his eyes caught something near the walkway far below.

"What do you see?" asked Grace. All three girls saw the expression on Isaac's face as he jerked the binoculars back up to eye level.

"Not sure, but I thought I saw something... er, ah, some-one."

"Who? Who?" The girls clammered for an answer.

"Noooo!" Isaac curled his mouth into an "O" and blew air through his lips. "No way!" His mouth fell open as he mumbled: "It's Spike."

~~~

"No way!" Andrew couldn't believe what his grandfather had just read. "How did Spike get all the way down to the water. I mean... Never mind, I know he made it out of the lava tube several minutes before them. But," continued Andrew, who was now sitting straight up in bed. "I still can't believe he just left his friends like that!"

Andrew began to ask what Spike was doing at the shore-line, but his grandfather simply started reading again and Andrew did not want to miss a word. He quickly zipped his lips.

~~~

"No, wait." Isaac's voice became very serious. He began to yell Spike's name as loud as he could. Then he stopped. "Something is wrong." Isaac turned and snapped the order to "wait here" at the three girls. He then started off in a full sprint down the road toward the walkway and ocean far below.

"I'll never make it in time," Isaac thought to himself while running. He was weak and tired and his legs seemed to move in slow motion. "Spike!" He yelled again and again, between his heavy panting. It was of little use. The water's edge was still hundreds of yards away.

Back up the road, Grace stood holding the hands of both Rebecca and Keiko. All three wondered what had gotten into Isaac. He made them very nervous and Rebecca eventually decided she would not wait any longer. With Isaac's figure becoming a smaller and smaller dot racing down the flat, black road, she informed the other girls that they should follow. Grace said that it was not a good idea. Isaac, after all, was pretty clear that they should wait. But, the girls did not like being left alone and Rebecca still hoped her parents were down at the walkway by the ocean. Perhaps they were with Spike, she prayed.

What made Isaac run and act so strangely was what he had seen behind Spike. The shoreline of the ocean had receded far out from where it was supposed to be. He could see dry land where there should be water…for quite some distance. Isaac knew what this meant – a tsunami was heading for land. He knew that the power of a large tsunami pulled the ocean out to sea moments before it made landfall. This was similar to the gravitational pull of the moon when it caused low and high tides.

Isaac had covered the distance of a few football fields but he was not yet there. Not even close. Spike did not hear him as he wandered off shore onto the now-dry rocks that had only moments earlier been under water. Isaac was out of breath and panting so heavily as he ran that his voice was barely audible even to him. There was no sign of anyone else. Just the two cars, huts, and walkway at the end of the road. And Spike, who was now probably fifty yards off shore and still walking.

And then Isaac saw it.

The wave was so large that it was not so much a wave as it was the entire ocean heaving upward. Up and up it rose as if the whole earth were sinking. Even the sky seemed to drop and darken. The site made Isaac dizzy and then he had a horrible sinking feeling in his stomach. The wave would destroy everything in its path, including him.

Fear swept through Isaac's body and paralyzed him. He stood still for a full fifteen seconds. He stared at the wave which continued to grow, rushing forward at an alarming rate, forceful, angry, and unstoppable. It was the horrible sound that snapped Isaac out of it. He recognized the sound as the sound of a large locomotive train running at full speed nearby.

Isaac squeezed his eyes shut hard and realized there could not possibly be a train where he was standing. As his mind processed the reality that the sound was not a train but the sound of the monstrous wave, Isaac's body responded. He turned and ran as fast as his legs would carry him back up the mountain road.

"Run!" Isaac yelled repeatedly, hoping the girls would hear him. The grade of the uphill road had slowed Isaac's progress to little more than a fast walk. He dared not look over his shoulder. The locomotive sound grew deafening and Isaac feared it was already upon him. He wanted to turn and look for Spike but, instead, he willed himself to run faster, repeating the words to himself. "Run, run, run." It seemed to help.

There, before him in the distance were the girls. They were perhaps three football fields away, small figures still holding hands and walking toward him. "Why didn't they listen to me?" Isaac's brain screamed over and over. Fear washed over Isaac and he found himself dripping with sweat and unable to think straight. But his legs continued to churn. The only thought in his mind was, "The wave would hit Rebecca and it would be my fault!"

"RUN!" Isaac screamed. This time it came out louder than anything he had managed in his life. He repeated: "RUN!"

They saw him. Grace's mouth fell open. Rebecca must have seen the wave because she pointed past Isaac in the direction of the ocean. Her mouth was moving. Obviously she was shouting something back toward him, but Isaac could not hear a word. He continued screaming "RUN!" and began flailing his arms wildly in a motion saying "get away!" The girls got the message. They turned and started to run also.

Isaac did not think it was possible for the roar of the locomotive to be any louder. But he was wrong. The sound was so overwhelming that it had the effect of almost knocking Isaac off balance as he ran. He was sure the wave was overhead and instinctively turned and glanced back toward the water. As soon as he did, he wished he hadn't. The wave was making landfall only a thousand feet below and its size doubled from what he had seen earlier. The height of tidal waves always increased as they made landfall. The rising ocean now boiled over powerfully with whitecaps and a violent frothing and foaming of water.

There was no sign of Spike. Isaac turned back around and ran faster than he ever ran in his life. He did not realize it but he began to cry as he ran.

~~~

"Grandpa, the tsunami will catch Isaac!" Andrew's hands cupped his face and his mouth fell open. "He can't outrun it."

"No one can outrun a tsunami, Andrew. This one was moving at over a hundred miles per hour."

"Spike?" Andrew knew the answer and his grandfather simply shook his head from side to side.

The old man set the book down and spoke in a calm voice. "Is this too upsetting for you, Andrew? I'm sorry, Tiger. Maybe I shouldn't be reading this to you this late at night."

"No, no!" Andrew protested.

"But maybe I should …"

Andrew interrupted his grandfather. "I have to know what happened to Isaac. Did he make it?"

"Right, okay," agreed the old man. "Isaac lives. I'll tell you that part but then we are stopping for the night."

~~~

Isaac did not think he would live. This was it. He had covered some ground up the sloping hill but felt the tsunami behind him. And then he felt the water push him violently forward off his feet. "Run!" As the word left his mouth, Isaac choked hard on water. He was spinning wildly out of control in the wave and his mind could not discern up from down. This was it. And everything went black.

Chapter 11

Devastation

His face ached terribly. Reflexively, Isaac put his hand to his nose and the pain that seared through his body cleared his mind. Isaac shook his head and coughed violently, spitting out putrid water and salt. "Am I alive?" He obviously was because of the taste of water and vomit in his mouth. The pain from his nose spread throughout his face every time he coughed. He opened his eyes but did not recognize anything. The sun blinded him temporarily. "It is daytime," Isaac thought to himself.

"Oh, no! Rebecca!" Isaac pushed himself up to a sitting position, managing to suppress the scream building up in his throat from the pain.

He was splayed sideways on the road. It was the same road he had been on earlier. Now he recognized where he was. Isaac was back near the parking lot of the lava tube where he started. The wave must have carried him the short distance back up the hill. Isaac probably should have counted his blessings. The chance of surviving the ordeal of being scooped up by a racing tsunami are one in a million, but he did not have time to contemplate the miracle. He had to find Rebecca and the girls.

As Isaac slowly and awkwardly stood up, he nearly blacked out again. What Isaac did not know was that the wave completely destroyed the coastline and everything in its path. It raced several hundred yards up the hill but, by the time it hit Isaac, it was only a few feet high. It had carried him only about the length of a football field, bounced him off a tree alongside the road, breaking his nose in the process, and rolled him onto his side in the middle of the road. He was saved by the steep incline of the sides of the volcano. Had it been flat ground, the wave would have traveled another mile inland. He was also saved by luck.

This was not the main tsunami, but the first of two large waves and several small ones. And it was not the worst of them.

~~~

Isaac stood in the middle of the road. His hair and shirt were dry, meaning he had been unconscious for at least as long as it took for the sun to dry his soaked body. Looking down the hill toward the ocean, the site he saw unnerved him. There was absolutely no sign of the tiki huts and parking lot by the coast. Huge boulders and rocks had been pushed by the wave across the landscape, and now sprawled unnaturally in every direction, while the few palms that dotted the coastline were knocked flat. The entire shelf that made up the side of the volcano leading down to the water dropped several feet. Isaac could not be sure of this, but it certainly appeared as if the land had dropped away during the earthquake.

As he raised his hand to shield his eyes from the sun he was again reminded of his broken nose. The realization that he had been knocked out for at least a few minutes or maybe even an hour worried Isaac. What had happened to Rebecca and the girls? The sun was still high in the sky, so it could not have been too long, he realized. And Isaac set off in a slow, limping jog up the hill to where he had last seen his sister.

As he called out his sister's name, Isaac recalled watching a documentary on television about tsunamis. It was this documentary that led him to run when he saw that the tide had receded far out into the ocean because he knew that was an indicator a tsunami was on the way. Had he not run he likely would not have survived the wave.

"Rebecca!" Each time he called out his sister's name his nose hurt and he felt as if he would black out again. But the thought that tsunamis often came in groups of wave after wave gave him the strength to keep moving forward up the hill. Isaac was also thirsty, but he did not stop to drink water. Instinctively, he reached up and patted the straps of his backpack, as if to reassure himself that it was still on his back.

"Incredible," he thought to himself. The backpack stayed put while he was somersaulted in the wave. Thankfully, he had worn his hiking pack with straps that both crossed his shoulders and connected around his waist.

The sun was so bright in the sky that, if not for the signs of devastation all around, it would be hard to believe a massive wave had roared across the land only moments earlier. It was clear that the water had crested just prior to hitting the lava tube. The dense vegetation and large fern trees that marked the entrance to the lava tube still stood untouched. However, the car that had sunk part way down into the gash in the ground was nearly out of sight. The earthquake must have opened the gash a few feet across and only the fender and lights of the car were visible above the hole in the parking lot. The earth was slowly digesting the car.

It was this scene that reminded Isaac of the Okinakas still stranded in the lava tube. If another wave came, one that might travel higher up the volcano's slopes, and if they were still in the lava tube, they would be drowned inside the cave. Isaac was torn as to whether to keep looking for his sister, Grace, and Keiko, or to warn the Okinakas. He literally took a step toward the lava tube, then stopped and took a few steps away from it, before sighing heavily and hustling up the small knoll atop the lava tube.

It was no use trying to use the entrance. That had been blocked. There was no way he was going to get back into the lava tube. Then Isaac remembered something he had dreamt.

The details were foggy, but he recalled the large, Hawaiian lady from the luau – the one with the big wrap-around dress and hair like fire. She pointed back behind him and up the slight sloping hill. What was her name? It was right on the end of Isaac's tongue but he could not remember it. Isaac shook his head from side to side, trying to wipe the cloudy dream from his mind and focus. But, as he did, he felt the urge to turn and look over his shoulder.

That was it! Isaac remembered the small opening in the ground from where he and the girls had climbed to freedom when they escaped the lava tube. He wondered in disbelief at the thought that his blurry dream about the old Hawaiian woman had told him how to get back into the lava tube. "That couldn't be possible," he thought to himself. But he headed toward the opening. As long as the pile of rocks from the collapsed roof had not moved he could climb down them and re-enter the tube. As he looked for the opening, Isaac continued to call out for his sister, the girls, and his parents. He caught himself just as he was about to yell...

~~~

"Spike." Andrew's grandfather paused after he mentioned the name. He had that far-off look again.

"What?" Andrew asked. "What is it, Grandpa? Did Spike make it?"

The old man told his grandson that Isaac had wondered

why his friend had walked to the water by himself, and the thought angered him. Of course, Spike would have had no chance at all, he explained. He was too far off the coast when the wave rushed in at great speed. "There was no outrunning a tsunami," he explained.

"Except for Isaac," corrected Andrew.

"Well, that was dumb luck. The wave had nearly run out of steam and Isaac was just lucky he had not made it down to the water's edge before it hit. If he had…"

Andrew's grandfather let the thought hang while he took a long, slow drink from his cup of tea. Andrew understood perfectly what might have happened. He wanted to ask his grandfather about Rebecca, Grace, and Keiko, but he was afraid of the answer he might get.

Instead, his grandfather said simply, "Malamalama."

"Hmmm," murmured Andrew.

"Malama. That was the name of the old lady from the luau. The one from Isaac's dreams," explained his grandfather. "The name he couldn't remember."

"Ah, come on, Grandpa. That's silly. A dream that is real?" But Andrew's own voice seemed less certain that the dream was silly.

~~~

Isaac nearly tripped over a small branch that had fallen off a tree. Just a few feet beyond the fallen branch he spotted the hole that led down into the lava tube. It was the same one through which he had crawled not long before. Isaac peered down into the hole. It was so black that he could not see more than a few feet. It looked as if the pile of rocks was no longer there so he removed his backpack and fished around for his flashlight. Everything inside the pack felt soggy and musty. Grabbing the flashlight, Isaac splayed out on his stomach. With his head and right arm down into the hole he turned the flashlight on. It worked!

One of the reasons Isaac had bought it before the trip was because it claimed to be waterproof. "Who would ever have thought I would actually need a waterproof flashlight," he chuckled out loud. His words echoed down into the lava tube. Sure enough, the rocks were still there. The beam of light showed the ten foot high mound just below his outstretched arm.

As Isaac zipped up his backpack and prepared to descend into the lava tube, he remembered that Mr. Okinaka had a broken leg. The fallen branch he had nearly tripped over a minute ago might come in handy as a crutch. So, Isaac quickly retrieved it, threw it down into the lava tube, and began lowering his legs down to the mound of rocks.

It was a frightening feeling. He remembered all too well what had nearly happened in the tube. Not once but twice had the rocks crashed down from the ceiling. "What if there is another earthquake when I am in the tube?" Isaac was murmuring to himself, and scaring himself in the process. "This time I would be alone. What if another wave came…?"

"Hello –"

The word echoed but only slightly in the cave. Isaac realized he had better concentrate on each step while descending the pile of rocks. Twice he nearly lost his footing and small rocks cascaded down the mound, cracking loudly as they hit the floor below. The flashlight was barely of any use. The lava tube seemed darker than before and Isaac imagined he was not alone. His fear was playing games on him. He imagined horrible beasts hiding in the cave. Isaac nervously and quickly picked up the branch and felt the need to swing it violently from side to side, as if to lash out at any of those beasts lurking in the dark just beyond the reach of his flashlight.

Isaac's chest heaved from his panicked breathing and he realized he needed to calm himself down and quickly find the Okinakas. "There is no such thing as monsters in a cave." He repeated the words over and over, straightened his back, and moved as quickly as possible through the cave in the direction where he last saw the Okinakas.

Not five minutes into his search he heard Mrs. Okinaka say, with much anxiety, "Who is it?"

The couple was a short distance from where he had last seen them before he and the girls departed. As soon as Isaac answered, Mrs. Okinaka gasped. She blurted out something in Japanese then, catching herself, repeated the words in English. "Where is Keiko? Is she alright?"

"Yes, yes." Isaac assured Mrs. Okinaka, not sure if his voice gave away the worry he felt inside. He was glad that

Mrs. Okinaka could not see his face in the dark. As he explained that the girls had run from the tsunami and that he had been caught in it, Mrs. Okinaka reached out and grabbed his arm. She squeezed tighter and tighter as he told her what had happened. Of course he omitted the part about not finding them after the tsunami.

Yoshi Okinaka interrupted several times. He was obviously concerned about his daughter and wanted his wife to interpret what Isaac was saying every few words.

"Look!" Isaac finally stated firmly. "We must get out of here. Now! The roof could collapse at any moment and there may be another wave! The last one nearly made it to this spot."

"I know," Mrs. Okinaka was struggling to regain her composure and calm. "We felt the horrible ..." she paused while trying to think of the right word.

"Shaking?" Isaac finished her sentence.

Mrs. Okinaka finished, nodding her head in agreement. Her husband pointed beyond Isaac and spoke quickly and sternly in Japanese.

"Yes," Mrs. Okinaka changed her thought. "We knew we had to get out. My husband is in much pain. He cannot walk but he is trying. He wants to know if there is a way out behind you."

"Yes, but he will have to climb." And with that, Isaac handed Mr. Okinaka the branch. He did not need to explain its purpose because Yoshi Okinaka immediately put it under his arm, leaned heavily on it and struggled a step or two forward.

"My husband says 'go' and we will follow."

It was slow going. Mr. Okinaka grimaced and nearly fell after each step. Isaac prayed that the branch wouldn't break, that his flashlight wouldn't fail, or that there would not be another quake. They were moving much too slowly. Much too slowly.

"Hurry," Isaac was restless. "We've got to get out of here and get Keiko."

Mrs. Okinaka did not need to translate. Isaac saw the man bite down hard, fix his eyes forward, and pull his broken leg across the rocks and water that littered the entire floor.

It took entirely too long to climb the rocks. Yoshi Okinaka slipped several times when trying to pull his bad leg up the pile. Each time he grunted in pain.

~~~

"They'd better hurry." Andrew was upset. "Why doesn't Isaac just leave them? Another wave is coming!"

"Well, they needed his help. They didn't have a flashlight. The small pen light Isaac left with them was nearly useless in the pitch black tube."

Andrew shook his head in agreement, but added "I know, but it is taking too long to get out."

~~~

Isaac was the first out of the cave and then helped pull

both Okinakas out of the hole. When they were all back on the surface of the knoll, Mrs. Okinaka gasped and held Isaac's shoulders. In the light of day she saw the damage to his nose.

"Your nose. Isaac, are you alright?" Her face gave away her concern.

Both Isaac's eyes were bloodshot and black-and-blue circles stretched upward from his nose to both eyes. He looked like he had been punched twice in the face. He felt like it too. But Isaac told her he was fine and that they needed to get to higher ground and meet up with the girls.

When Mrs. Okinaka asked him where the girls were, Isaac fibbed and said that they were just around the bend and near the Visitor Center, which was only a short distance up the hill. He was not sure if Mrs. Okinaka bought it or not, but either way all three of them struggled forward. Isaac turned and started down the knoll to the lava tube's parking lot. He could not help himself. He started to run.

"Go!" It was Yoshi Okinaka. Yoshi understood Isaac's urgency. He followed the word with a wave of his hand and a few words in Japanese.

Mrs. Okinaka agreed with her husband. "You need to run, Isaac. Go and be with Keiko and the other girls. We will only slow you down and Yoshi remembers the way up to the Visitor Center. We will meet you there."

Isaac did not say a word. He simply started running. Each step resulted in a searing pain in his nose, but the thought of losing his sister drove him onward. He hoped the girls were safe.

Chapter 12

⊕

Survivors

Fortunately, when the girls saw the tsunami coming, Grace grabbed Rebecca by her good arm and almost pulled her up the road. Both girls had seen Isaac in the distance, running and waving his hands frantically at them to "go!" They also saw the wave even while it was still out at sea. How could they miss it? It was the height of a tall tree.

It is not easy to run with a fractured wrist and Rebecca screamed and cried the whole way up the road. Keiko had not seen the wave, but she followed the two older girls, alarmed by the panic in their voices and actions. She actually ran ahead of them, as Rebecca struggled with each step. Fortunately, the wave literally poured itself out at their feet, running its course near the parking lot of the lava tube.

After the water crested behind them, the girls stopped running but kept walking. They all wanted to look for Isaac but Grace would not let them stop. Exhausted but alive, by the late afternoon the girls had made it past the lava tube and were nearly to the Visitor Center before they sat down under a tree. Grace wisely made the girls stick to the road. She figured it was their best chance to find Rebecca's parents or be rescued.

Safe, at least for the moment, Rebecca and Keiko soon fell asleep in the shade. Sleep, however, did not come to Grace. She was too worried and was still looking for Isaac. Tears welled up in the corners of Grace's eyes as she thought of Isaac getting swept away by the wave. That was the last sight of him before she turned her head, pulled Rebecca forward, and ran for her life.

~~~

Isaac had struggled for several minutes to cross the gash in the road that cut across the entrance to the parking lot of the lava tube. The worst of the quakes had dropped the one side of the small road – the side closest to the ocean – a full three feet. Isaac could not have known it but the entire shelf of the volcano had dropped several feet into the sea. The force of the quake had also pulled the shelf several feet out toward the ocean, leaving a gaping wound in the earth.

Isaac navigated the jagged tear with great care. He contemplated jumping across it. But, after measuring the distance with his eye, he decided that, while the length was doable, the problem was the height of the opposite side of the gash. The three-foot-high ledge meant that he not only had to jump *across* a few feet but simultaneously jump *up* a few feet. But, climbing across it was also dicey. He decided to jump.

After jumping across the gash, Isaac crashed into the opposite wall. He held on with his arms while his legs, dangling in the hole, then dug into the rock wall for a toe-hold but the rocks under his feet twice gave way. The second time this happened Isaac fell hard against the wall and the sharp lava rock gave him a cut across his shin to match the wound across his knee from his fall in the lava tube. But he eventually made it across. He did not know it but not far from that very spot the gaping hole closed and the road came together, allowing someone simply to step across it. This was the very location the girls had crossed earlier during their way back up the volcano.

As Isaac lifted his exhausted and aching body up out of the trench, he heard a roar coming from the direction of the ocean. The sound cleared his foggy thoughts and Isaac immediately swung his backpack off his shoulder and dug into the contents looking for his binoculars. They were nowhere inside the backpack. Isaac dumped the contents on the ground and tore through the items splayed out before him, looking for the binoculars. Then he remembered that he was holding them in his hand while running toward the ocean to save Spike. When the wave overcame him and spun him through the water, he must have dropped the binoculars.

Isaac stood, leaving the contents on the ground in front of him, rubbed his eyes and strained in the direction of the sea. He was so tired that everything seemed to be blurred. Fortunately, the late afternoon sun was behind him, which allowed him to look eastward toward the ocean. There it was. Another wave.

The monstrous wall of water raced toward the shoreline and looked even larger than the previous one. "Not again!" Isaac's exhaustion did not turn to fear or panic, but to anger. The events of the day now made him feel as though he could face and handle anything, but he was angry that he had to deal with another problem. Inside his head he heard Malama, the old woman from the luau, telling him to run but not to worry. He would be safe.

Because the wave looked bigger, Isaac knew it would come farther ashore. With a quick, sweeping motion, Isaac's hand pushed all the objects of his backpack into the main compartment. He began running, zipping the bag shut as he ran, shaking his head to rid himself of the thoughts of the old woman. A few items from the pack fell to the ground, but Issac did not stop. With a quick swing over his arm, he threw the bag onto his back as he ran.

Several times while running, Isaac felt like stopping and simply facing the wave. He had never been this tired before in his life. He also nearly tripped a few times. But he kept on running and running. As he ran he hoped the Okinakas had made it across the gash in the earth and that the girls had made it to higher ground farther up the volcano. And his parents… Isaac did not allow himself to think of what had happened to them. Rather, he just kept running.

~~~

A little farther up the volcano, Grace also heard the roar of the wave. She stood but could not see it over the strange formations of lava that dotted that part of the volcano. Standing like statues and large pieces of furniture, dark lava mounds rose up at odd angles in every possible shape and size. Grace climbed the nearest one and saw it. The wave was huge, larger than the other one, and was nearing landfall.

It took her three tries, but Grace eventually was able to wake up Rebecca. Neither Rebecca nor Keiko really seemed to understand what she said to them. They were more asleep than awake and, like zombies, moved slowly up the road. Grace yelled, pushed, and pulled the girls but little she did helped. She began crying as she realized that they might be moving too slowly to escape the wave. They had been lucky with the first wave but Grace did not want to try their luck again. "Come on, hurry! Please!" Grace pleaded through her tears with her friend and the little girl from Japan. "Hurry!"

Grace looked over her shoulder every few steps. She saw the wave burst high into white foam as it crashed into the shoreline. But the land did not even slow it. The wave continued on as if it were determined to destroy her. "Hurry!" she screamed again. The wave continued racing across the land and the sound grew louder and louder. The locomotive was coming again.

"Hurry! Hurry!" Grace pleaded with her friends. Nothing she did helped. Keiko's body seemed to be made of Jell-O and she slumped forward after each step. Rebecca's eyes remained closed as she shuffled her feet forward, more asleep than awake.

"Hurry!" Grace was pulling both girls by the arms.

~~~

Tired hardly described how Isaac felt. The stress of enduring earthquakes, lava tubes, and tsunamis for hours on end had left him deliriously exhausted. He managed to keep going, however. The thought of Rebecca and the girls being swept away by the wave kept him moving. He was running at a decent pace up the road toward the Visitor Center.

Isaac scanned the black lava fields for signs of the girls. It was easy to do because the area was largely without trees and most anything stood out against the pitch black rock. As he called out their names, it finally dawned on him. The water from the first wave had crested just prior to the lava tube and the road under his feet was dry. Everything around him was dry. This meant that the tsunami had not reached this high. His mind raced with the ramifications of this discovery.

On one hand, if the girls had made it this high they would have been safe. On the other hand, maybe he was looking in the wrong direction. If the girls had been swept up in the wave, the receding water may have carried them back down toward the ocean. If that had happened, Isaac was looking in the wrong place.

Isaac was so tired that he could not think clearly to make a decision. Should he run back toward the coming tsunami to look for them? For several seconds Isaac stood motionless screaming the names of the girls. "Rebecca! Grace! Keiko!" he yelled as loud as his burning lungs would allow. He did so until he had trouble breathing.

He began to panic. But Isaac's will to survive took over and he began running again, farther up the middle of the road toward the Visitor Center and away from the coming tsunami. All the while, he heard the crashing and roaring of the wave behind him.

Isaac again tested the limits of fate and luck. As he ran, he heard the sound of the wave drawing closer and closer until the sound quieted and grew softer and softer. He did not look back. He did not need to. He knew he had made it again – just as the voice of Malama had told him. But he was also too tired to look back.

Isaac shuffled slowly to the side of the road, his body functioning on auto-pilot. He did manage a clear thought: I need to sit down for a few minutes to clear my head. The thought repeated itself in his head as Isaac knelt down in a cradle of a large boulder by the side of the road. The rays of the late afternoon sun, shining in at an angle, poured over Isaac's body as he curled into the side of the boulder. He was fast asleep before he realized what he was doing. His last conscious thought was that this had to be the worst day of his life. The worst of anyone's life.

~~~

"But he was so close to Rebecca and the girls! Didn't he know they were not far away?" Andrew's tone revealed his disappointment in Isaac not finding Rebecca.

"One-half mile to be exact," said his grandfather. "The girls were only a short distance up the road. You know, Andrew, enduring one hour of a very stressful experience is utterly exhausting. But Isaac had cheated death the entire day."

"But he was so close. Couldn't he go a little farther up the road?"

"No," said Grandpa. "Isaac had summoned a strength he never knew he had, and he did this the entire day. Few people could have done what he had done. At that point he slept. It was a deeper sleep than he had ever experienced. In fact, he slept straight through the night, barely even moving."

"The whole night!" Andrew was more disappointed than surprised.

"Yes, and it was a good thing. He would need the rest because of what was in store for him the next day."

Chapter 13

Visitors

Malamalama, the heavy lady with the hair like fire, spoke to Isaac. Though her mouth did not move, Isaac knew she was telling him to be strong. She was chanting something but Isaac did not understand the words. They were in Hawaiian. From all around her flames from a fire flashed in bursts of heat and bright light. Lava bubbled beneath her feet. Isaac could feel the heat. It grew hotter and hotter. He was now sweating from every pore in his body and the lava crept closer and closer toward his feet. Isaac looked up from the lava as he stepped backward. Malama's chant grew louder and louder to the point where it was becoming frightening. She seemed possessed. Her body wriggled and moved with the beat of drums and gurgling of lava. Suddenly, everything stopped. Malama stared at Isaac, crossed her arms like an "X" in front of her, and said "Kapu! Be careful. Evil comes."

Isaac's eyes opened wide as he snapped out of a deep sleep. He awakened feeling worse than he ever imagined someone could feel. His entire body ached and was so stiff he had trouble standing straight. He winced in pain as he straightened his back and looked up into the bright sunlight. It was morning. The position of the sun in the sky indicated that it was not too early, nor too late in the morning. He had been dreaming. Again.

Isaac dreamed of the mysterious old woman from the luau. She seemed to be teaching him in his dreams. He remembered her making him watch as Kalani, the large, friendly Hawaiian he had met at the luau, slammed the coconut down on a sharp spike in the ground, then twisted the fruit until it opened. Isaac had the sense that, in his dreams, Malama was pleased that he had watched the two men getting and opening the coconut.

Isaac coughed violently and, when he did, his broken nose throbbed with pain. His head pounded and felt as if it had been used as a punching bag. Both his knee and shin were swollen and discolored. Dried blood was caked on the wounds. At some point in the night he must have removed his backpack and used it for a pillow. But it did little to alleviate the pain in his neck and head.

But he was alive.

Isaac had slept through the entire night and struggled to remember what he had last been doing before sleep overcame him. He remembered rescuing the Okinakas from the lava tube and remembered crossing the gaping hole in the road. Yes, the pain in his shin reminded him of where he had fallen while trying to cross the tear in the earth. Without thinking he reached down to his throbbing shin. When he brought his hand back up he saw red. He had rubbed the large scab which had formed while he slept, and now his shin had a trickle of blood across the purple-colored swelling that covered the front of his lower leg. It hurt.

As Isaac fished a bottle of water out of his backpack to take a much-needed drink, he finally remembered running from the second wave. "Wow, was I lucky," he thought to himself as he swirled the water in his mouth before swallowing it. His mouth was dry and the water did little to quench his thirst. He also felt his lips. They were chapped and somewhat sunburned. They too hurt as he took another drink. In fact, everything hurt.

Isaac was disciplined, taking only two relatively small sips of water. Putting the bottle back into his backpack, he threw the pack over his right shoulder and began walking back up the road toward the Visitor Center. His steps were slow and painful. Fortunately, there were no more signs of tremors in the earth and no more sounds of giant waves. "Perhaps we're finally done with all that," he mused, shaking his head in relief of the promise of no further natural disasters.

Isaac walked for no more than ten minutes before he heard one of the most deeply satisfying sounds of his life. It was Rebecca and Grace calling out his name. Looking up from the road he saw the three girls running toward him from the bend just a short distance up the hill.

As thrilled as he was, Isaac lacked the energy to run to meet them. He simply removed his backpack, smiled a toothy grin, and opened his arms to await them. Moments later Grace crashed heavily into him, squeezing him so hard that he grimaced and felt it in his aching back. Keiko held Rebecca's hand but they too eventually gave him a hug. Isaac never thought he would mind hugging his sister, except for the time of her medical emergency a few years earlier. Rebecca still wore Isaac's shirt around her neck, rigged to act like a sling for her fractured wrist.

"Aren't we a mess!" Isaac laughed. The girls nodded in agreement.

"Isaac, look at your nose! What happened?" Rebecca made a face of disgust and started to reach up as if to touch her brother's crooked nose.

Isaac caught her hand with his.

"Does it hurt?" asked Grace.

"'Course it does." Isaac managed a wincing smile.

"Gross nose or not, I'm really glad to see you, Isaac." Isaac could tell that his sister meant it.

"Yeah," it was Grace. "We thought, er, I mean, I thought you... I mean I saw the wave hit you." Tears welled up in her eyes.

Isaac told the girls how he broke his nose while being tossed about in the wave but how he somehow managed to survive it.

"Here," said Isaac, unzipping his backpack and handing Grace a granola bar. "Split it. There are only two left after this one." He also handed Keiko the water bottle he had opened not long before.

As the three girls inhaled their portions of the granola bar and water, Isaac told Keiko that he had found her parents and that they had made it out of the lava tube. But, he admitted that he lost them when he ran ahead to try and find the girls. He felt somehow as if he had abandoned the Okinakas, so he apologized to Keiko. Only after doing so did he realize that the apology might be taken as a sign that the Okinakas did not make it through the last tsunami. So, Isaac explained himself again, telling Keiko that her parents were alright but that he did not know where they were because he had fallen asleep.

"They said we should meet up at the Welcome, or ah, the Visitor Center up the hill," he explained to Keiko and the others.

"I'm still hungry, Isaac," said Rebecca. The other girls nodded in agreement.

"Me too," agreed Isaac. He never thought it possible to be this hungry. "But we have to ration our food. We have to save it. I think we'll be okay now, but just in case."

"But I'm really hungry. I could eat a cow." Rebecca's silly expression made everyone laugh. They all laughed too hard at her choice of words, and did so because everyone really needed to laugh. They all thought that they might not see one another again. It was a nervous but relieved laugh.

"Well," smiled Isaac. "We had better start looking for a cow!"

"I'd settle for McDonald's," grinned Grace.

But her comment made the kids remember what had happened to Spike the day before. It was Spike who always wanted to eat at McDonald's and always said he preferred the Golden Arches to whatever any of them wanted. The three older kids seemed to get the reference at the same time because all three of them stopped joking. Keiko just looked slowly and curiously up at each of them, one at a time, as if to ask what she had missed.

It was Isaac who broke the moment of silence. "Did you see anyone up the road?" He looked at Grace.

"No. No one at all." Her tone turned serious.

"Did you make it all the way up to the Visitor Center?" He looked back and forth from Grace to Rebecca.

They both shook their heads 'no.'

"Well," continued Isaac. "I don't know if Keiko's parents are still below us." He pointed down toward the lava tube and ocean. "Or, whether they are above us by the Visitor Center. But we should go up the hill to the Center. Plus," he said reassuring himself of his decision, "it is near the main road."

"Do you think there'll be more earthquakes or waves?" asked Rebecca.

"Hard to tell, Becca, but if I had to guess, I think we've seen the last of the tsunamis." Isaac patted his sister on the shoulder as she leaned into his chest. "But I think we ought to try and get ourselves rescued."

"We have to find my mother and father," pleaded Keiko.

"Yes, I agree," echoed Rebecca. "We need to find our parents too."

"Yea." Isaac and Grace spoke in unison.

"Well, I think our best bet is to get moving," Isaac pointed up the road. "It can't be more than a short walk to the Visitor Center. Maybe a few minutes. I don't know." He was thinking out loud. In truth, he did not know how far it was but he remembered it was only minutes by car.

"That's right," agreed Grace. "There's gotta be people there. Maybe your parents. Yours too!" She looked at Keiko with a comforting smile.

"And they will have food and water," said Rebecca.

"Maybe even a cow," teased Isaac. "Let's go."

And so the four children started up the road, walking in a tight pack and with thoughts of what they wanted for lunch in their minds. Being back together as a group seemed to reassure all of them. Isaac smiled and promised that he would never leave his sister again. No matter what.

~~~

After walking for several minutes, the girls were tired of walking. Isaac had to admit that he was tired too. And they were all hungry. The lack of food and water along with the glare of the hot sun had sapped their energy. Grace pointed out to Isaac where the girls had spent the night and he could not believe how close they were to one another last night. "If only I had made it a bit farther up the road," he thought to himself.

They saw a sign on the side of the road for the Visitor Center. It was straight up the road. All four kids cheered and hugged when they saw the sign. Even though they were close, Isaac agreed that they should rest. They did, finding shade under a tree beside the road. It was clear that Rebecca's wrist was really bothering her and his own body was still painfully sore. Although, he noticed that the pain went away a bit when he read the sign on the side of the road.

As they sat under a small grove of juvenile palms, Isaac told everyone to take off their shoes and air out their feet. It dawned on him that he had slept in his shoes the night before and that his feet could be added to his growing list of sore body parts. So, he thought, maybe the girls too had slept in their shoes. Collectively, everyone let out an "ahhh" sound when they took off their shoes and stretched out under the palms. Rebecca's feet had pink blisters forming across the heels and tops of her feet and she grimaced as she rubbed them.

The sun was rising and it was starting to get hot, but it was not yet too hot. The late morning was warm, but bearable.

"So, what are you going to eat when we are rescued?" asked Grace.

"Yea, what's it gonna be, Sis?" Isaac chimed in, winking at his sister.

"Well, first I'm gonna drink three cans of Sprite. Then I'm gonna get a shower."

Isaac interrupted his sister. "We all could use a shower!"

"Yea," agreed Grace, "then how about we order room service? I want to just relax in my bed the whole day and watch TV!"

"And eat," reminded Rebecca. "First thing I'm gettin' is ice cream. Then I'll get a huge burger with extra cheese."

"That would be nice," smiled Grace.

"Yum!" Isaac felt the inside of his mouth water at the thought. "Man, I'm really starving," he thought. "All this talk of food is makin' me hungry. What do you all say – let's go!"

As the kids started standing up, a thick voice startled them. Rebecca even let out a small scream in alarm.

~~~

"Where ya think you're goin'?" The voice was deep and slow, so slow that each kid had turned to see who was talking to them before the big man finished the sentence.

Standing behind them on the road was a mountain of a man wearing a bright orange jump suit with the sleeves cut out. Isaac immediately noticed the tattoos. One on each forearm. One had a dagger through a bleeding heart and the other had a map of the Hawaiian islands.

Keiko and Rebecca started backing up. Fear swept over

them. They were both inching backward down the road. Isaac and Grace made eye contact, eyes wide as if to ask "Should we run?"

"Not so fast." From the other direction a smaller man started to laugh. He reached out and grabbed Keiko by the shoulder. She shuddered and clenched her eyes shut.

"Stay awhile," the man grunted.

The voice was menacing and Isaac felt his heart skip a beat and his mouth go dry. He could not believe who he was looking at. It was the same man he had seen on the chain gang alongside the road when the family was driving to the volcano. The big man was the prisoner who was entering the prison bus when Isaac's father drove by. Isaac remembered how the entire mini-bus leaned when the huge man walked up the steps.

The big man let out a roaring laugh at his partner's "stay awhile" comment. He was missing two teeth, but Isaac did not notice because he could not take his eyes off the small man behind them. The smaller of the two men had a heavy beard stubble and was no longer wearing his orange prison clothing. Instead, he was wearing the uniform of a police officer, however it was ill-fitting and perhaps two sizes too big. The collar was unbuttoned and the shirt not tucked in. From under the shirt, Isaac could make out a large, black holster on the man's hip and could see the butt of a pistol sticking sideways out of the un-tucked shirt. Isaac also saw what looked like a blood stain on the collar of the shirt.

But what Isaac and the girls most noticed was a long scar, stretching from the man's forehead nearly to his chin. It split what should have been his eye but was now a milky, lifeless ball.

~~~

"No way, Grandpa! It's the same man with the scar from the bus!" Andrew shook his head from side to side with surprise and concern. "How is that possible? I mean, he was part of that prison gang, right? He was being guarded by the police."

"Yea, you're right, Andy." Andrew's grandfather also seemed upset. The expression on his face gave away his mood. "Well, you see, the prison bus wrecked when the worst earthquake struck. Ran off the road into a ditch. Two of the inmates, the bus driver, and one of the guards were hurt pretty bad. As soon as it happened, the small inmate, Scar, grabbed the gun from the injured guard and..." Grandpa paused for a moment, thinking of the right words. He continued, "Uh, Scar was able to take care of the other officer."

"No way!" Andrew repeated himself, then mumbled the expression over and over as his grandfather continued.

"The guard had the keys to unlock the shackles on each prisoner. So Scar was able to free himself and the other convicts."

"But what happened to the other police officer and the

driver?" asked Andrew. "And where are the other, um…"

"Prisoners?" His grandfather paused, took a deep breath, and continued. "Yea, well, they weren't coming to the volcano. But Scar and his partner, Tiny, had made their way to the Visitor Center where they broke into the vending machines and stole the money from the cash register."

"But what about the park ranger, Grandpa? I mean, isn't there a ranger when you go to national parks?"

"There is, but…" Again, Andrew's grandfather paused. "Scar surprised him and stole what he needed."

"What about his friend? Why didn't he take one of the uniforms for tiny?" Andrew asked.

"Ha! Good luck," his grandfather answered. "Tiny couldn't fit in any of them. He'd need to sew two uniforms together! Now, where was I?"

~~~

"Uh huh," said Scar, noticing that the kids were staring at his eye. "An unfortunate situation. Call it an occupational hazard." He pointed at his eye, then reached into the shirt pocket and pulled out a pair of sunglasses, which he very slowly and deliberately put on. Before he did, he winked at Isaac with his good eye then slipped on the sunglasses. After he pushed the sunglasses up his rather pointed nose, Scar let out a snarling laugh.

"Occupational hazard! D'ya like that one, Tiny?" The

smaller man smiled at his bigger companion. A frightening grin spread slowly across his face.

"Good one, boss," bellowed the big oaf. "You da kine! You da man! Eh, you crack me up!"

Keiko still stood by Scar's side. She was squeezing her eyes shut but did not move. Scar let go of her shirt sleeve and patted her on the head. Keiko's eyelids shut even tighter.

"Let her go." Isaac was surprised that he summoned the courage to speak to the small but dangerous man, but he was upset that his voice quivered with nervousness. It therefore lacked the firmness to be convincing.

"Tell you what, little Bro," said Scar, still smiling. "When you have the gun, you get to make the decisions. Comprende?"

Chapter 14

Trouble

That quickly, a gun flashed. In a blur, Scar pulled the weapon from the holstered pistol and now held it at Keiko's head. Isaac's mouth dropped. He felt paralyzed with fear.

"Tell you what, Bro." Scar twirled the pistol around in his hand, slowly pointing it at Keiko then at Isaac, then at each of the girls. "This is how its gonna be. And I'm only gonna say this one time, got it?"

Isaac did not know if he had said something or if he had nodded his head or not. He remained frozen.

Then Scar smiled again. "You don't call the shots. I call the shots." Then he looked at the big oaf and grinned, "Get it? I call the *shots*. Like that one, Tiny?"

"Good one, boss. Da shots. Like a gun, huh?" Tiny's huge stomach rolled as he laughed. "Yea, kid, da boss call da shots.

Get it, kid? Boss, you crack me up!"

"Give me your backpack." Scar pointed the pistol in Isaac's direction. "Now." His one eyebrow raised above the top of the sunglasses to put an exclamation point behind the request.

Isaac did not want to lose his backpack. It had their water and the last of the granola bars in it. But he slowly removed it and held it in front of him.

"Get it." Scar nodded his head in Tiny's direction.

The man was huge. As he leaned down to grab the backpack from Isaac's hand, Isaac could not believe how big he was. This man was the biggest person he had ever seen. Even bigger than Kalani. His meaty hand was over twice the size of Isaac's. Tiny did not take the backpack from Isaac, he tore it out of Isaac's hand and opened it upside down. The contents spilled across the pavement below. Water bottles. Granola bars. A soggy, torn map. Journal. A pencil that was now broken into three pieces... And Isaac's pocket knife. It slid across the pavement and landed near Isaac's shoe. Quickly, Isaac put his foot over the knife, hiding it. The knife folded into a compact unit and therefore was easy to hide. Isaac hoped the two prisoners had not seen what he had done.

Scar was not paying attention. He had pushed Keiko away and smiled as she fell to the ground. Grace ran a few steps to Keiko's side and hugged the little girl. The distraction allowed Isaac to get away with his risky move to hide the knife.

"What we got here?" Tiny picked up the unused water

thermos, unscrewed the cap, and raised it to his lips. In three giant gulps, he drained the contents, spilling a little of it, which trickled down his fat chin.

"What's the matter with you?" Scar was angry and marched over to his big friend. In a lightening-quick move, he slapped the giant across the mouth. The thermos flew from Tiny's hand and spun wildly across the paved surface to the shoulder of the road. Isaac didn't watch what happened next. He grabbed the knife under his foot and quickly slid it into his pocket.

"Huh?" This was all Tiny mustered. He held out his hands, palms up as if to ask what he had done.

"Are you completely dumb? We've gotta save water. Don't drink it." Scar's smile was gone. He was no longer in a mood to toy with his captives. He was no longer the comedian. "Put everything back in the backpack." He was looking directly at Isaac, who complied and retrieved each item. "Tiny, split the water supply," ordered Scar.

The big man did not seem to understand the order, shrugging his shoulders as he began to ask a question.

"We've gotta save water for now. Take some of the bottles out of your bag and give them to the kid. He'll do the carryin' for us." Scar returned his gaze to Isaac.

Tiny apologized and did as he was told. He had a large, duffle bag over his shoulder. It was filled with candy bars, chips, and soft drinks that they had looted from the vending machine at the Visitor Center. He placed a few items in Isaac's backpack. As he was doing so, Scar spoke.

"That ain't for you to use. Any of ya'll. If I find that you touched any of that stuff…" He let the word trail off, but waved the pistol above his head. "Got me?"

"But we're really hungry." It was Grace.

"I can cure that," said Scar. All four of the kids understood the message. They starred at his pistol. Scar smiled again and holstered the pistol, trying to spin the handle around like they did in the movies but botching the effort. He grunted, then announced: "Two other rules. One: No one touches this bag." He held up a smaller bag, something a tourist might use to bring supplies along for a day at the volcano. Then he tied the string of the bag to his belt.

~~~

"What was in the bag, Grandpa?"

Andrew's grandfather made the universal sign for money, rubbing his middle finger and thumb together.

"Ah, so that is the money Scar stole from the park ranger, er, I mean the Visitor Center?" Andrew nodded his head in the affirmative, pleased that he had figured out what was in the bag – with a little prompting from his grandfather, of course. "But, what was the last rule Scar mentioned?"

Andrew's grandfather removed his glasses and rubbed his eyes slowly. Then he rubbed his crooked nose at the point where it bent to the side and said, "Well, let's see what that last rule was."

"And the other rule is to keep your mouths shut. You see," Scar explained with a smirk. "Me and Tiny here. We gotta keep movin' for the next few days. He's my prisoner." Scar touched the badge on the police uniform he wore. "Officer Kelley." He read the badge, looking down at it. "Yea, I'm Officer Kelly, and this here little fella is my prisoner. Prisoner 38455, also known as Tiny." Scar smiled at the game he was playing.

"Dats right. You heard da man!" Tiny laughed. "He's Officer Kelley. He's da po-lice." Tiny dragged the latter word out so much that spit squirted out between his two missing teeth. Both men laughed.

"Let's go." Scar gave the command. "Anyone who breaks any of the rules…" He again patted the pistol on his hip. "Anyone who tries to get away…" Isaac did not look at Scar but knew what he was doing and what he meant. Rather, Isaac was looking at the girls, trying to meet their gaze and offer them a comforting "look." Only Rebecca met his "look." Her eyes blinked nervously. Grace was still holding Keiko's hand.

~~~

The two escaped prisoners led the kids away from the Visitor Center. And away from the hope of seeing their parents

153

and being rescued. They walked down toward the ocean, bypassing the destruction of the tsunamis. Rocks, boulders, bent signs, and debris littered the roadway. Isaac wanted to tell Scar about the tsunamis and the threat of another one. But, he decided against speaking. His mind was racing with ideas: "Maybe if there was another wave it would help them to run and get away. Maybe."

The girls walked slowly. Rebecca's wrist was still bothering her and the more they walked the more her steps seemed to slow. Isaac figured it was the blisters on her feet. As they walked he tried to remember if he had any band-aids in his backpack. He remembered that he had packed a small first-aid kit but had already used the Band-Aids for Rebecca's cut. But, he had gauze. Isaac also reasoned that Scar was taking them away from the main highway and Visitor Center because he too was trying to get somewhere, and that somewhere was away from the law. And away from any people that might recognize him or be looking for the prisoners that escaped from the overturned bus.

Then, as if Scar had read Isaac's mind, he spoke. However, he directed his words at Tiny.

"Hey. Look. There it is." He pointed at a pathway, carved into the sharp lava rock. It was strewn with debris from the tsunamis but was still recognizable as a usable walkway.

"What?" was Tiny's reply.

"That ancient trail I told you about, fool!" This time, Tiny remembered. He smiled a semi-toothless grin.

"This trail is kapu to you." Now Scar turned and talked to Isaac, forewarning that "kapu" was a warning in Hawaiian that meant "no trespassing." He crossed his arms like an "X" in front of himself, just as Malama had done in Isaac's dream. "That means it is off limits for you," Scar said pointing at Isaac.

"Why?" This was all Isaac managed to say.

"You are a 'malihini' – a newcomer. You ain't from here." Scar continued, "See Bro, this is an ancient trail Hawaiians used to travel 'cross the island. Stay on the trail and you might still have feet to walk on!" Seeing the worried expressions on the kids' faces, Scar laughed at them. "See that sharp lava rock?" He pointed to a stretch of jagged black rock that looked more like a weapon than any stone Isaac had ever seen before. "That's a'a"..."

"Yea," interrupted Tiny. "See dem a'a! Dey cut da feet somethin' terrible! So, you betta listen to my Brah. He's da boss."

Isaac and the girls looked down at the black rock that stretched for miles from the side of the road. It looked sharp and was definitely something you did not want to step on.

"Yea, dats why dey call it a'a," boasted Tiny. He pointed at Isaac's shoes. "Cut dem shoes right off yo' feet. Quick like! Then you scream a'a!"

"Let's go. No one will come down here. Especially after those quakes and waves." Scar tired of the small talk and motioned to Tiny who turned off the road and started across

155

the ancient trail used by Hawaiians for centuries to cross the volcano. It was half as wide as a sidewalk and lined on either side by smaller rocks, although many of them had been washed away from the tsunami. On either side of the trail was the sharp lava rock called a'a. One by one the kids followed Tiny. Isaac looked down at the sharp rock but as he walked past Scar the two made eye contact. When they did, Scar again patted the butt of the pistol on his belt. And smiled. He then took his place at the rear of the line.

Chapter 15

Coconuts

Isaac was so tired that he had trouble focusing as he walked. He felt as if he were sleepwalking. And as he did, his mind wandered. Again, Malamalama filled his head. She reappeared, only this time they were all back at the luau. Malama instructed Isaac to watch the young Hawaiian man from the hotel luau who climbed the coconut tree. Isaac remembered seeing the young man with the machete clenched in his teeth climb the coconut tree. "Watch him. Learn." This was Malama's message. And Isaac did. The man shimmied up the tree with a rope tied from one ankle to the other. He seemed to climb forever. Higher and higher he went.

Then Malama pointed upward as the man reached the top of the tree. Silhouetted in a spotlight, the man very slowly raised the machete high over his head. Isaac did not dare blink, worried that he might miss what was coming. He remembered that night back at the resort when he watched the luau show. It seemed to be so long ago but it was just two days ago. Malama wanted Isaac to learn a lesson but she also had a warning for him. Then it happened. Quickly. The machete flashed through the night sky and severed the coconut from the tree. Whack!

Isaac snapped out of his daydream. He was still walking along the ancient volcanic trail. The small band walked for the remainder of the morning before stopping to rest. The sun had passed overhead, so Isaac knew the noon hour had come and gone. It was Rebecca who stopped the march across the ancient Hawaiian trail. She had mumbled a few times that she was tired and thirsty. Then, she simply stopped and sat down; or rather, she plopped down. Her head was hanging low, so low that her hair touched the ground in front of her. She had collapsed into a ball.

Isaac rushed up to her side and knelt down. He then turned and explained to Scar that Rebecca had broken her wrist and needed food and water. After Scar said nothing, Isaac repeated himself, then added that his sister also needed to get to a doctor. Grace and Keiko also joined Rebecca, kneeling by her side along the trail. Isaac un-slung the backpack and began unzipping it in order to get Rebecca something to drink and eat. He was also feeling around for his emergency first-aid kit containing the gauze for her blisters.

"'Eh, Bro, not so fast." It was Scar. He walked over to the kids and reached down to Isaac's pack. "I'll be takin' that,

Little Bro." Isaac clutched his backpack with all his strength and, for a moment, held on to it. Scar tugged but Isaac kept his grip on the pack. But, then Isaac felt the blow across his head. He did not even see it coming. Scar slapped Isaac hard across the top of the head with a half-closed fist. Isaac let go of the backpack without realizing it.

"I said, 'I'll be takin' that." Scar's tone was harsh; he was not smiling. Isaac could not hold Scar's gaze so he looked back down at Rebecca and squeezed her hand reassuringly. Blood pounded through his head where Scar had hit him. It stung sharply.

Without looking back up at Scar, Isaac said in a tired but firm voice, "She needs something to drink and eat. And she needs a doctor." He then added the word "Please." As soon as he said the word, he was not sure he should have pleaded with the frightening man with the pistol.

And then he heard the unmistakable sound of a pistol cocking. Scar stood over the four children and aimed the pistol at Rebecca.

"See, Bro, I've been rethinkin' my decision to bring you kids along. Don't see much use for ya anymore." The deadly smile returned and he said in a slow whisper, "Ya see, there's no one 'round here. No one at all. No one to hear me shoot you. Besides, me and Tiny, here, we got our special bag..." Scar pointed to the duffle bag with money, tied to his hip. "And now we've got your pack and supplies." Then Scar's voice grew louder and the smile again disappeared from his thin lips. "And I'm startin' to get real tired of you. Real tired!"

"Sure thing, Boss. Me too," chimed Tiny. "What we need d'ese kids for anyway?"

"Well, big fella, that's not for you to worry your little brain about. That was my decision to use them as hostages. 'Case we're caught…" Scar never took his eye off Isaac while he talked to Tiny, who stood a few feet ahead of them on the old trail. Then Scar realized that he was supposed to be pretending he was a police officer escorting his prisoner. "Er, ah, y'know – in case I run into more bad guys like you, Tiny. Remember, I'm the law here!"

"Oh yea, Boss," laughed Tiny, playing along with the joke that everyone knew was just that – a joke.

"But, enough of this dilly-dallyin' around!" Scar leaned forward and the pistol came closer toward Rebecca's head.

"No! Wait a minute!" yelled Isaac. "If you pull that trigger…" His voice trailed off.

Scar seemed a bit surprised at first, but then played along with Isaac, making fun of his show of courage. "Yea, then what? What you gonna do, little Bro?" That quickly, Scar's mood swung again. The man was unstable and dangerous. "What you gonna do when I pull this trigger?"

"Yea, what ya gonna do, Brah," repeated Tiny. But, for all his bluster, Isaac detected that Tiny was worried about what was happening.

Then a thought raced into Isaac's mind. And it came from

his daydream with Malama. "You need food, right?" Scar did not answer Isaac's question. "I can get you fresh coconuts. But, if you shoot my sister, I swear I'll not get you a single one. I'd rather die." Isaac felt a strength pouring over him. He slowly stood directly between Scar's pistol and Rebecca. Scar's gun was now pointing directly at his chest.

"So, you wanna make the call, do you?" Scar was angry. His face reddened and his hand trembled ever so slightly. Isaac could feel it as the barrel of the pistol rubbed across his chest. "What if I don't need no coconuts? We've got food in the bag!"

Scar inadvertently turned and looked at Tiny, who blurted out, "Ah, well, a few packs of crackers and chips, Boss."

"Zip it, fool." Scar was angry that Tiny revealed their situation. But he knew it was right. Then that horrible smile returned along with the calmness in his voice as Scar looked at Isaac, "You really ready to die, little Bro? Okay." And Scar pushed the pistol against Isaac's chest so hard that Isaac nearly tumbled over backward. But, he leaned into it and held his ground.

"If you shoot me, who'll climb those trees and get the coconuts?" Isaac pointed to his left and there, in the middle of the black a'a rock stood a small grove of coconut trees surrounded by the only stretch of sand in site. It was a salt and pepper, grainy sand, not like the sugary sand from the beach he had recently visited.

"I know how to climb a coconut tree."

"Ha!" Scar snarled. From behind Isaac, Tiny also laughed. Scar still held the pistol at Isaac's chest as he talked, "Bro, you tellin' me you can climb those trees? Ha! I'd like to see it." And Scar dropped the pistol, putting it back in the holster with one deliberate move.

"Man, Boss, dat boy's too skinny. No way he climb d'ose trees! No way!" Tiny was chuckling between each sentence and pointed to the trees. He then began to pretend he was climbing an imaginary tree, dancing about awkwardly. If Isaac was not so worried about the proposition he had just gotten himself into and what would happen to Rebecca – and the other girls – if he failed, he might have laughed at the big brute jumping up and down as if to grab a coconut in the sky.

Scar was amused. "Well, Bro, what're you waitin' for. Climb." He nodded toward the trees.

"Isaac." It was Grace. She had a worried look on her face and her eyes were tearing up. Rebecca remained in a lotus position, slumped over from exhaustion in the middle of the ancient trail.

Isaac turned and headed across the a'a lava toward the coconut trees a few feet away. His foot slipped off one of the sharp rocks, and raked across the corner of it, slicing his ankle slightly. Isaac closed his eyes and stood still, not wanting to show anyone behind him that he felt the searing tear. Now both his knees and legs were covered in dried cakes of blood, except for this fresh wound, which began trickling warm blood into his hiking shoe.

"Yea, boy, watch dem a'a!" It was Tiny. He had seen the slight slip and was roaring with laughter. "I told ya – dem a'a gonna get ya!"

Tiny continued his play-by-play commentary laughing about the a'a "gonna get ya" but Isaac ignored him and carefully crossed the lava field to the salt-and-pepper sand. From his vantage point below the trees, they now looked a lot taller to Isaac than they did earlier. He took a deep breath and clutched the tree with both palms of his hands, leaning his body backward so as to straighten his arms just like the young man from the luau had done when he climbed the coconut tree. Isaac began to climb. It was difficult and he nearly lost his grip several times, but he pushed hard with one foot after the other. Isaac was climbing the tree. His body sagged, as if he were sitting down, and his arms began to tremble slightly, but up he went. Isaac was about ten feet up the tree – about half the height of the trunk – and then he lost his grip and fell.

Isaac landed hard on his back. The air rushed out of his lungs and Isaac gulped in a panic, not able to get his breath. The force of impact had knocked the breath out of him. His ears seemed to fill with blood and they rang as he struggled to catch a breath, but he could hear the laughter nearby. Tiny and Scar were obviously enjoying his failure. Tiny had even pretended to fall on his back, mimicking Isaac's flop. After a full minute, the air began entering Isaac's lungs again, at first in spasms, but slowly his breathing returned to normal. Isaac winced in pain, finally realizing how hard he had landed. As he sat up, he looked to his left and then to his right. All around him was sharp lava rock. All around him, that is, except the spot on which he landed. It was padded with grainy but soft salt-and-pepper sand. Not a foot from where his head landed Isaac saw an especially menacing piece of a'a – about three feet high and sharp as a sword.

"Phew," Isaac exhaled and counted his blessings. Without realizing it, Isaac mumbled "thanks" to Malama, crediting her for helping him to avoid the sharp a'a rock. As he stood he remembered something from his dream. Isaac reached down and undid his belt. He then tied it carefully from one ankle to the other, lashing it tight. The distance between his feet and the outstretched, taut belt matched the thickness of the trunk of the coconut tree perfectly. This is what the man had done when he climbed the coconut tree at the luau. So, Isaac figured, it must be part of the proper technique.

Isaac braced both feet against the bottom of the tree, reached up with extended arms to get a grip around the thick bark, and then leaned back. He began climbing but fell again, this time only four feet up the tree.

But Isaac stood and immediately grabbed the tree. After a few awkward pulls and pushes, Isaac shut his eyes and concentrated. His motions smoothed out and the task, while painful and strenuous, felt natural to him. Lean back. Arms straight. Pressure against the tree from his feet. He did not know how he knew how the climb the tree. But he did. It was working! Isaac did not dare open his eyes until he felt he was nearing the top of the tree. Some five minutes had passed and Isaac's arms were beginning to quiver with muscle exhaustion. He opened his eyes.

There in front of him was the top of the coconut tree and a batch of six large, dusky-colored coconuts. Isaac contemplated reaching back to his back pocket and getting his pocket knife. It would help him cut through the lashing holding the coconuts to the tree. But then he thought better of it. He did not want Scar to know he had a knife. Instead, Isaac slowly leaned into the tree until his chest rested against the tree and his legs and one arm were wrapped around the trunk like a baby koala bear hugging its mother. Then he lost his grip and slid a foot down the tree. The bark scraped painfully against the skin on his exposed arms and legs. But, like a powerful snake squeezing its victim, Isaac squeezed with all his might, both legs and arms hugging the tree.

Once he was stable, Isaac slowly opened his eyes. He then released his grip with one hand and pulled on the closest coconut. Nothing happened and he quickly let go of it and clutched the tree, feeling like he was about to fall.

He tried it again, this time twisting the coconut slightly and letting his natural weight and gravity pull on the fruit. To his surprise, the coconut snapped free and fell to the ground below. It landed with a thud in the grainy sand, in the exact spot where Isaac had fallen earlier.

Grace and Keiko burst into an impulsive applause. He could hear them cheering, but returned his focus to the task at hand. One by one, Isaac, tugged and twisted each of the other five coconuts, freeing them from the top of the tree. One by one they fell with thuds to the ground. Two of them rolled onto the black lava rock but did not crack open. Grace and Keiko continued their cheering and Isaac thought he heard Scar talking, but he concentrated on getting back down the tree.

His first step downward missed the mark and Isaac slid a few feet down the tree, scraping his stomach against the rough bark as his T-shirt rolled up to his chest. Fortunately, his hands caught a grip on the trunk and stopped his quick descent. Isaac's arms, however, were shaking from muscle fatigue. He was exhausted and didn't believe he could hold on any longer. But, as he had done earlier when climbing the tree, Isaac closed his eyes and concentrated. He slowly slid down the tree a foot at a time, all four limbs hugged the trunk. When he was about five feet from the bottom he could hold on no longer, let go, and fell off balance to the ground below, landing on his side. But he did not feel a thing. He had done it. Through his heavy breathing from the physical exertion, Isaac smiled, proud of himself for what he had accomplished.

"Here," he said, through heaving breaths and staring straight at Scar, "dinner is served."

Scar shocked Isaac with his next response. "Well, bravo, Little Bro. Didn't think you had it in ya. Maybe you are a little bit Hawaiian, after all. Now, before I change my mind, pick up that fruit and let's eat."

Tiny hobbled across the a'a, complaining with each step and nearly falling twice. Isaac tried to ignore him and suppressed a laugh from deep within himself. Together the two of them – Isaac and Tiny – held six large, ripe coconuts, three each in cradled arms. Then, Scar's comment took the air out of the pride Isaac was feeling.

"Okay, Little Bro. Now watchya gonna do? You're the expert. How you gonna open those cocos?" Scar sat down on the trail behind the three girls and wiped the sweat off his forehead. He was enjoying himself, toying with Isaac and the other children. "Hey," he shouted, "you could always use Tiny's head to open those cocos," Scar joked. "That head's as thick as a coconut!"

Tiny laughed, but then quickly stopped when he almost lost his balance and fell on the a'a rock.

Isaac had not thought of how he would open the coconuts. They felt hard and impenetrable in his hands. But then he remembered how Kalani had opened them by crashing them down, bottom first, on a sharp stick and twisting. Isaac set the coconuts down beside his feet and began to look around for a large, sharpened stick. There was debris from the tsunami strewn about the ground, including some litter from humans and a few palm fronds. But no stick. He reflexively reached around to his back pocket and nearly pulled the pocket knife out, but then caught himself and, instead, simply scratched his lower back for a minute while thinking. He needed something sharp to use to open the hard casings.

"We need a sharp stick. Like a stake," Isaac announced.

"Ain't no stakes here, Little Bro," grinned Scar. "You think you're at a hotel luau?" Scar taunted Isaac then started teasing Tiny that they really were going to have to use his thick head.

Then it came to Isaac.

The three-foot high lava rock he had nearly landed on when he fell out of the coconut tree looked sharp. It came to a thick, twisting point at the top. Without saying a word, Isaac grabbed the biggest of the coconuts and walked back to the lava rock near the trees. He steadied the coconut in his hands and, without realizing it, found himself quietly asking Malama to help him to open the husk. Raising the coconut high overhead, Isaac stared at the sharp point of the a'a rock and whispered "please, Malama, please." He then brought the coconut down in a violent jerk using all his strength. To his amazement, the coconut impaled itself on the rock!

Milky liquid oozed from the cracked bottom of the coconut as Isaac stared at the miracle before him. That quickly, Tiny, who had followed Isaac, shoved Isaac to the side. The bump nearly knocked Isaac to the ground, and Tiny grabbed the coconut, turned it upside down, and raised it to his lips. He slurped loudly and enthusiastically at the coconut milk inside the husk.

"Boss," Tiny crowed, face covered in white milk, "dis coco's ono-licious!" Isaac remembered that "ono" was the Hawaiian word for tasty. Kalani had taught him that.

"Well, go on, Bro," Scar yelled out, still seated on the ground. "Open the rest." He seemed neither angry nor appreciative. Rather, he was calmly resting on the trail, leaning back on one elbow and rubbing his bald head.

"Yeah," Tiny agreed, his face still in the middle of the coconut, "You da Hawaiian! Ey' Boss, da skinny Brah is Hawaiian after all!"

Scar did not answer.

Isaac did as he was told. One by one, he opened the coconuts, just as he had the first one. The fourth coconut cracked the sharp point of the a'a lava rock and Isaac had to find another nearby sharp rock. He took the second coconut to Rebecca and held her head as he poured the coconut milk into her mouth. She coughed and gagged slightly, but then drank it. Grace assisted her.

Isaac was surprised that Scar did not snatch the coconut for himself. Rather, he had stretched completely out on the trail and seemed to be dozing off. He said only, "Save the coconut meat for me. I don't like the milk."

The four children and their two kidnappers enjoyed the coconuts. Every bit of the milk and the white coconut meat was consumed. They were all very hungry. A few minutes after finishing the coconuts, Scar stretched back out on the trail, placed his forearm over his eyes to shield them from the sun, and ordered Isaac back up the tree to fetch more coconuts. Isaac complied. He fell twice but fetched a few more coconuts.

~~~

"No way, Grandpa! Isaac is Hawaiian!" Andrew was giddy with excitement. "He showed Scar, didn't he, Grandpa. Sure did!"

"Yes, Tiger, he sure did. And he surprised himself."

"Was it the old lady who helped him? The one from the luau at the hotel?" Andrew asked.

"You mean Malamalama?" Andrew's grandfather smiled as he spoke. "Well, that was just a dream, Andy. Hocus pocus. You don't believe in some kind of ancient Hawaiian magic, do you?"

"No, Grandpa, of course not. But…"

Chapter 16

☆ ☆ ☆

Stars

By the late afternoon the four children and their two captors had made it to the remains of a small village. The few houses of the village had been overrun by molten lava many years earlier. Where a small village once stood, now there was only several feet of hardened, black lava. Nothing stopped the advance of lava.

The small party finally stopped to catch their breath. Grace found herself standing on what seemed to be the rusted roof of an old car stuck buried in four feet of lava. Rebecca had regained a bit of her strength. Even though Scar occasionally made comments that sent a shiver down each child's spine, he did not oppose when Isaac walked beside Rebecca in order to assist her. Just as Isaac was about to request that they stop, Scar announced that they would spend the night here.

Without saying much, Scar motioned for Isaac and Rebecca to sit next to an old, rusty stop sign. Only the red octagon and a few inches of the pole below it were visible above the old lava flow. Isaac smiled at the thought of seeing the stop sign he had seen in photographs. He had always wanted to visit this place of destruction, but just not in this way. Scar ordered Isaac and Rebecca to sit and put their hands behind their backs. While they did, Scar slowly removed the bag of money from his hip. Using the rope from the bag, he tied Isaac's hands to Rebecca's, but Rebecca let out a cry. Her wrist was swollen two times its original size and was a purple-ish color. Seeing her wrist, Scar made a snide comment about the pain she must be feeling and how he doubted her wrist would ever be good again. But, he realized she would not be able to put her broken wrist behind her back, so he tied only her one good hand to Isaac's two hands.

Scar then removed Isaac's belt and, with brother and sister's hands behind their backs, Scar tied them to the base of the stop sign. It hurt a little and the position was uncomfortable. Isaac and Rebecca were side-by-side, sitting on the top of the mound of hardened lava, with their backs leaning against the stop sign.

Scar had made the kids carry the second batch of coconuts that Isaac had picked. They had carried them all day across the ancient Hawaiian trail. Now that they had stopped for the night, Scar ordered Tiny to collect the coconuts so that none of the kids would try to open or eat one at night.

"Now listen up," Scar announced to his four hostages, "When I wake up in the morning, all these coconuts had better be right here. No eatin' them! And that goes for you, too, Tiny!"

As Tiny huddled the coconuts together nearby, Scar grabbed Tiny's stash of food they had stolen from the Visitor Center and opened a few bags of crackers. None were offered to the children and Scar made exaggerated signs of enjoying the snacks while he ate them. Tiny joined Scar, eating three bags of chips himself before Scar snatched the pack from him and closed it. Isaac's mouth watered but he immediately looked away and helped Rebecca try to get comfortable.

As the sun settled low in the sky, Scar reminded the children not to even think about getting away. "Or else," he added. He smiled and patted the butt of his pistol. Grace and Keiko were trying to get comfortable on top of the roof of the old car. Grace's hands were tied behind her back using the police belt Scar was wearing, and she was lashed to the windowless door of the old car. Keiko sat beside her but was not tied. Scar looked directly at Keiko when he spoke, scaring the young girl into not trying to escape. Within a few minutes, Isaac and Rebecca heard Tiny snoring. They were all exhausted from the long walk and stress of never knowing when Scar would snap, but Tiny's loud snorting and sawing was going to make it tough to fall asleep.

A few minutes later, Isaac heard Grace and Keiko moaning and complaining in their sleep. The two of them fell into a deep but nightmare-filled sleep despite Tiny's snoring. Isaac, however, was unable to sleep. Not only was he hungry and sitting at an odd angle against the old stop sign, but Rebecca was uncomfortable too. She repeatedly whispered to Isaac that she wanted to free her good arm in order to help cradle her injured wrist. All the walking on the uneven trail and two days without ice or medical treatment had left her wrist badly swollen and sore.

As Isaac tried to comfort Rebecca, he recalled that fateful day a few years ago when his sister had almost died. Perhaps it was the predicament in which he found himself or it might have been the emotion of having Rebecca so close to him and in so much pain, but the details of that day came flooding back to Isaac.

It had been a bright, spring morning, the kind of day that feels like the seasons were changing with the welcoming of summer. With the wet, sweet smell of freshly cut grass in the air, Isaac had run out of the house and had forgotten to close the front door. Only days earlier he had received a bicycle for his birthday.

Eager to keep up with her big brother and see him on his bike, Rebecca chased out the front door of the Sanders' home and, without looking, crossed the street. Isaac was peddling away from the house and toward the sidewalk on the opposite side of the street. It was when he rolled up onto the sidewalk that he heard the sudden and slight screech of tires as the driver of the car locked his breaks in an effort to avoid hitting Rebecca. It did not work. Isaac would never forget the sinking feeling in his stomach as he turned and saw Rebecca stretched awkwardly on the road in front of the car.

That quickly, Isaac's mother came sprinting out of their house and the driver – Mr. Tanner, who lived at the end of the block – threw his door open and jumped out of the car. Fortunately, the car had been traveling slowly along the small road that winded through the neighborhood. Rebecca's hip was fractured where she was struck by the grill of the old car and two ribs along with her wrist were broken when she was slammed onto the road.

Sitting beside Rebecca, tied to the old stop sign, Isaac looked down at that same wrist that was now broken for a second time. He never liked hugging his sister – or any display of affection, for that matter – but he wished his hands were free in order to help comfort her at that moment. Isaac had always blamed himself for the accident, even if his parents never said the obvious. It was a very painful and frightening lesson to learn and the pangs of guilt were never far from Isaac's thoughts during Rebecca's long and slow recovery. In truth, these feelings never truly disappeared.

John and Clara Sanders became overly protective of Rebecca after the accident and Isaac developed a sense of responsibility for his younger sister. While other kids in school often refused to be seen with younger siblings, for instance, Isaac still walked to and from school each day with Rebecca… and always would.

Isaac leaned his head as far down toward Rebecca as he could and whispered to her that he was very sorry about that accident a few years back, and was equally sorry he could not protect her during her fall in the lava tube. He need not have bothered to apologize. Rebecca was asleep, breathing in spasms as her head rolled gently from side to side. Isaac did not know why, but he repeated himself even if his sister would not hear it.

It was going to be difficult to sleep and Isaac vowed to himself that if they made it through the ordeal – "No," he reminded himself, "*when* they made it back safely," he would never again take for granted the comfort of a bed and pillow. Isaac drifted off to sleep to the soothing but spectacular sight of a thousand twinkling stars. It was like sleeping in a planetarium. The clear skies over the middle of the Pacific Ocean and total lack of lighting from any nearby homes and cities produced a magical show in the night sky. He slept fitfully that night, waking up in pain and discomfort. So too was he visited by the old lady from the luau. Malamalama haunted Isaac's dreams for a third night in a row. Somehow, however, her presence was reassuring to him.

~~~

"What did Isaac dream about, Grandpa? Did Malama tell him how to get away from Scar or how to beat him?"

Andrew's grandfather took a deep sip from his tea and

grinned. "In fact, that is exactly what Isaac dreamed about. You see, the Malama visited him again that night, as she had been doing each night in his dreams. This time she told Isaac to bring Scar to her, that she would 'take care of' Scar for Isaac."

"But, where does Malama live?" Andrew asked. "Must they go back to the resort where they saw her in the luau?"

"No, Andrew. That was not really Malamalama at the luau. It was the spirit of the great Hawaiian goddess, Madam Pele, appearing as Malama."

"The god of fire and volcanoes, right?" Andrew had excitedly blurted out the answer.

"Well, yes, Andrew, but she is a goddess, not god. The Hawaiians believe she lives in a large volcanic crater called Halema'uma'u. It is a lava-filled crater on the slope of Kilaueau Volcano and the Volcanoes National Park."

Andrew was a bit confused about the lady at the luau not actually being Malama, but rather the spirit of Madam Pele. Andrew's grandfather recognized his grandson's perplexed expression, so he explained...

"Well, you see, Andy, the Hawaiians believe the spirit of Madam Pele can take a human form. So, it would seem that she appeared at the luau as Malamalama."

Andrew nodded his head in the affirmative. He was beginning to understand. "Could the others tell that she – Malama – was Madam Pele?"

"No, they couldn't. Only Isaac. You see, Madam Pele

took a liking to Isaac. She must have realized that Isaac loved Hawaii and respected the ancient Hawaiian traditions."

Andrew again interrupted, "Because Isaac wanted to learn all about Hawaii, right Grandpa? And, unlike Spike, he wanted to wear a flower lei and go to the luau and stuff, huh? So, what's going to happen? Is Madam Pele going to help Isaac?"

"Well, let's see what this old book says…" And Isaac's grandfather picked the book back up and continued reading.

Chapter 17

Crater

Isaac awoke to a loud, powerful sound. In the fog of sleep, his first thought was that another tsunami was hitting. He could hear the dull, thudding sound directly over him. He opened his eyes, blinked sharply at the bright morning light, and looked up into the blinding sun. Directly overhead was a helicopter.

It took Isaac a few seconds to register what it was and what it meant to have a helicopter flying overhead. He opened his mouth to yell, but his voice was dry and weak. Barely a sound escaped his lips. Isaac swallowed hard – how he wished he had a glass of water or, better yet, a tall, cold glass of orange juice. His mouth watered, giving him a voice. "Here!"

A calloused hand snapped quickly across Isaac's mouth. It was Scar.

"Shhh, Bro. We wouldn't want that chopper seein' us,

now would we?" Scar was kneeling down by the stop sign behind Isaac and Rebecca, but his eyes never left the helicopter flying low overhead.

Isaac struggled for a moment. It was useless. His hands were tied behind his back and then affixed to the old stop sign. Both his arms had the tingling feeling of being asleep. Then Isaac realized the helicopter could not have heard him anyway. He quickly glanced over to Grace and Keiko. If he could make eye contact with them and get Keiko to wave her arms overhead or run, maybe, just maybe the pilot would see them.

Neither girl was anywhere to be found. Isaac scanned the surface of the black lava, supressing the feeling of panic. Then he saw Grace. She was being held tightly by Tiny, who hid below one of the few trees standing in the old town. In the shade of the tree, Tiny's bright orange jump suit was only somewhat visible. "And Keiko?" Isaac thought to himself. "Where is she?"

Isaac began to panic. Where was Keiko? His sister was still asleep beside him and her face was very pale. She did not look good. And the helicopter was beginning to move away from them. "No," he thought, "it could not leave. They had to be rescued."

Isaac bit down hard on Scar's finger across his mouth and Scar let out a wincing sound. That quickly, Isaac screamed as loud as he could: "Here! We're he…"

Crack! Scar's half-closed hand came down hard across

Isaac's head, knocking him into Rebecca. Rebecca cried out as Isaac landed on her swollen wrist, which rested in her lap. She awoke in pain, her eyes indicating she did not remember where she was.

"Don't ever!" Scar had his bitten finger in his own mouth, nursing it. He removed it. "Never try that again!" And he reached down and grabbed Isaac by the neck, choking him. "Never."

Isaac said nothing and Rebecca began to cry. Scar turned his gaze to Rebecca and Isaac could see that the rage was welling up inside the menacing little man.

"I won't. You have my word." Isaac tried to distract Scar, drawing his attention away from Rebecca, who was sobbing. It worked. Scar gave Isaac a stern look, pointed at him, then stood and seemed to forget Rebecca.

"That was close." Scar motioned to Tiny, then looked upward at the helicopter as it flew away, becoming less and less visible in the morning sky.

"Too close, Boss," was Tiny's answer. "Who d'ya think it was? Da po-lice?"

"Doesn't matter." Scar stood for a moment. "Let's get goin'. I wanna put some distance 'tween us and this old town. Gives me chicken-skin, anyway."

Scar motioned to Tiny, who brought Grace back over to the stop sign where Isaac and Rebecca sat. Isaac saw the worry in Grace's eyes, but did not dare saying anything at the moment. The giant man bent down on one thick knee and pulled loose the belt and rope used to tie Isaac and his sister to the old sign. As the children fell free of their binding, Isaac rolled onto his side and massaged his aching wrists and shoulders. Rebecca let out a sharp shriek, then curled forward into a ball. She sat still for a few minutes while Isaac struggled to stand up. His entire body ached and he had been bitten by mosquitoes that night. Small, red bumps dotted his exposed arms and legs.

"Pick up those coconuts and let's get goin'" commanded Scar. A candy bar flew from his hand, passing over Isaac's head. Tiny's fat paw shot out and grabbed it in midair.

"Touchdown, Boss. Yea, Bruddah!" And Tiny danced his version of a touchdown celebration. "You know it!" He smiled at Isaac, then opened the candy bar and stuffed the entire thing into his mouth. "Ono-licious, little Brah."

As the children stood, with Isaac helping Rebecca to her feet, Isaac could stand it no longer. "Where's Keiko?"

Scar did not answer him. He simply turned and started walking along the ancient Hawaiian trail. Grace made eye contact with Isaac and she shrugged her shoulders as if to say, "Don't ask me? I don't know." As Isaac turned and began looking around the landscape, Tiny pushed him in the back.

The three children fell into line behind Scar, with Tiny bringing up the rear, humming an unrecognizable song to himself…and doing it off-key. The five of them walked for about twenty minutes without saying a word, Isaac and Grace carrying the spare stash of coconuts Isaac had retrieved the day prior. Then Scar stopped. He looked to his left, then to his right, and repeated the gesture for a few minutes.

"Which way, Boss?" Tiny asked.

"Shut up. I'm thinkin'," answered Scar.

Isaac noticed that the old trail simply ended. The old lava flow that covered the town or the recent tsunami had erased it from the face of the earth. Isaac's dream from the night before came rushing back to him in vivid detail. Suddenly, he was glad Scar was stumped and felt that perhaps Malama had done it. Maybe she had removed the old trail.

"The trail just up and ends. Makes no sense." Scar was talking to himself. "How could it just stop?" He then slowly turned around and looked at the three children as if they had somehow removed the trail at night. After a few seconds he yelled to Tiny to throw him a bottle of water. Tiny fished in the burlap sack filled with the loot they robbed from the vending machine at the Visitor Center.

"Here, Boss." And he tossed Scar a can of what looked like a Sprite.

"I said 'water'," Scar grimaced at Tiny as he caught the can and spun it around in his hand.

"Sorry, Boss. We flat outta water."

As Scar opened the can, the warm contents spewed out in a small explosion, startling him and soaking his arm. Isaac wanted to laugh but bit his lip and only smiled at Grace. Scar pretended the explosion had not bothered him, slowly took a long drink from the can, then spoke.

"No one said anything 'bout the trail endin'." Again, he spoke mostly to himself. Then he turned and again surveyed the land in front of him.

And that was when Isaac had an idea. It was from his dream. He had to get Scar to go to the Halema'uma'u Crater, which, if he remembered correctly, was up the volcano and away from the coastline beside them. Of course, Isaac thought, he could not simply tell Scar to go there. He swallowed hard, and tried to even his voice before talking.

"Me, I'd stay by the coastline." Isaac was pleased with how calm and natural he sounded. Scar did not respond. He did not even turn around. But Isaac continued. "There's bound to be some boats that come by. Maybe the Coast Guard or the police. Up the mountain there are more trees and cover but…"

Scar cut Isaac off in mid-sentence, but did not turn around. He spoke with his back turned to the rest of his party. "So, you're callin' the shots, little Bro? I thought we'd been through this before? You think I don't know 'bout the boats and the forest up mauka?" "Mauka" was the Hawaiian word for going up a mountain. He took another long drink from the can, draining the contents then took a long look at the coastline below. He then crushed the can in his hand, dropped it on the ground, and continued. "No, Bro, somethin' tells me we should head up the volcano. It's cooler and more shade. Plus, I call the shots." And Scar patted the butt of the pistol on his hip.

Then, Scar finally turned around to face Isaac. "Unless you'd like to stay here." He glanced at the pistol, threatening Isaac. Isaac said nothing. He understood the meaning. Then Scar said what Isaac had been wanting to ask. "Your little Asian sistah..." He paused as if to torture Isaac and Grace, who leaned forward in anticipation of what he was about to say.

"Yea," Scar continued. "Your little Asian sistah, she disappeared."

"What do you mean, disappeared?" It was Grace. Her voice reveled her concern.

"Just that," Scar shrugged his shoulders. "Must've been in the middle of the night. Coconut head, over there," Scar spit while he motioned to Tiny, "was supposed to be keepin' watch. But he fell asleep."

"Boss..." Tiny began to explain, but Scar cut him off.

"Yea, ol' Coconut head was too busy sleepin' and sawing down half the island with his snorin'. He was supposed to be keepin' watch." Scar then turned around and started to walk up the sloping side of the large volcano. "No matter. She's good as dead out here. No water. No map." He shook his head as if pretending to be upset at the thought of what faced Keiko. "Plus, if ya get off the trail where the lava crust is fresh or thin..."

And Scar stopped talking and just walked up the hill. Isaac and Grace looked at one another with concern. "What had he meant," their expressions asked one another.

Tiny answered, "Yea, betta be watchin' out. Fresh lava's got da thin crust. If ya step on it…" Tiny brought his finger across his throat, as if pretending to slit his own throat. "You no mo'. Wanna know why?" He had both Isaac and Grace's attention. "Cuz, ya fall through dat thin crust. Straight through. And ya know what's down there? Hot lava. Hotta den hell."

Tiny laughed loudly, obviously pleased that he had scared his prisoners.

Scar said nothing. Out in front of the others, he walked up the sloping volcano toward where he thought there would be shade and trees. But, as Isaac had remembered from the park map he studied, the hill would lead them to the Halema'uma'u Crater… just like Malamalama had told him in the dream.

~~~

"So, Grandpa, Isaac and Malama are going to get Scar now?" Andrew answered his own question by saying, "I bet they are!"

"Well," Andrew's grandfather answered, "it was tough going. They were off the ancient trail, which meant they had to cross the sharp a'a rock. And they had to climb 2,000 feet up to the rim of the volcano."

"Wow," exhaled Andrew.

"Yea, tell me about it. It was a difficult hike, and Rebecca was not doing well at all. In fact, Isaac worried that Scar would run out of patience because Rebecca kept lagging far behind the others." Andrew's grandfather had stopped reading and was speaking as if from memory. "And the strenuous hike was taking a toll on Scar's temper. At one point, when Scar stopped to rest, Isaac quickly suggested that he could open the spare coconuts for everyone."

"What did Scar say?" asked Andrew.

"Nothing. Nothing at all," responded the old man. "So, Isaac simply found a large, sharp piece of a'a rock and opened the coconuts. Tiny devoured his and me and Grace helped – I mean, Isaac and Grace helped Rebecca drink the milk, while sharing some of the white meat between them. Scar didn't eat anything. He simply sat on the trail and said nothing."

"Why, Grandpa? Why didn't he eat something or say anything?"

"I don't know, Andy. But he was always a lot scarier when he said nothing."

~~~

After a day of hiking, the small party climbed over a hill and arrived at a large crater – about the size of the soccer field behind Isaac's home back in Florida. It was shaped like a bowl. Slight cracks in the earth dotted the landscape and from each of them hot steam pillowed up into the air before disappearing skyward. Isaac could smell the sulfur as soon as they crested the small hill.

During the hike, Rebecca said little and Isaac did his best

to push her to keep up with Scar. He could tell that Scar was getting annoyed at the slow pace, at the difficulty of climbing uphill, and at not knowing where he was going. Isaac did not want to give Scar any reason to get angry with him or the girls. They had said little, even when they stopped to drink the dwindling supply of beverages Tiny carried in a large sack. Isaac and the girls were forced to split one can during their first stop, and Scar offered them nothing on the second break from the hike.

The sharp a'a had taken a toll on all of them, and when they stopped for a second time Isaac noticed that Grace's sneakers had started tearing. One of them looked as if it would soon fall off her foot. Grace caught Isaac staring at her sneakers and saw his worried expression. With a gentle raising of the eyebrows, Isaac motioned for Grace to be careful. If her shoes tore open Isaac worried that she would not be able to go on. The lava rock was just too sharp and treacherous. And there was no telling what Scar would do if one of the kids could not keep up with him.

Isaac looked over his shoulder at Tiny, who was sprawled out on his back. Somehow he managed to get comfortable on the rocks. Isaac realized that, had it not been for Tiny, the kids could not have kept up with the pace set by Scar. Rebecca was walking like a zombie, head down, feet dragging. But, Tiny was clearly winded and lagged even farther behind, bringing up the rear of the party. He was sweating so badly that it poured over his round head and his orange jump suit was a shade darker because it was covered in perspiration.

After a short rest, Scar stood and put his hands on his hips, staring blankly at the large crater. He looked confused and agitated. Rebecca and Grace noticed the pungent smell. Rebecca tried covering her nose with her hand and Grace crinkled up her nose at the stench. Isaac whispered to the girls, informing them to try to avoid smelling the sulfur directly.

Then Scar finally spoke. He was not happy and accused Isaac of tricking him, which, of course, Isaac had done. Scar did not look at Isaac, but demanded to know where they were. Isaac played dumb, then eventually suggested that they were at Halema'uma'u, one of the best known calderas of the park. Had Scar bothered to look, he would have seen the sign by the small parking lot informing visitors of the name of the crater. Scar did not respond and Isaac realized he was in trouble, so he added for effect, "I thought there was supposed to be a forest around here. But, look, it is a bit farther up the volcano."

It did not come out as innocently as he had planned it. Instead, Isaac sounded smug and victorious. Scar barked orders at Tiny to be on the watch. He warned that tourists or a rescue party might be near such a popular attraction. His words made all three children scan the horizon looking for people. After a full minute, Tiny broke the silence. His voice was weak as he responded that he saw no one. It was obvious he was very tired. Then he asked the question that had been hanging in the air like a weight about to fall: "So, what we do now?"

Without answering, Scar turned and walked aggressively toward Isaac and grabbed him by the arm. "Come on!" was all he said. Scar led Isaac across the flat lava field to the edge of the crater, pulling him violently as they walked. Tiny begrudgingly stood and pushed the two girls forward to follow his volatile boss. When Scar and Isaac reached the rim of the crater, Scar pushed Isaac in the chest, knocking him down.

"You played me, Little Bro," he snarled. "Ya got me to come here. You wanted me to come here? Didn't ya?"

Isaac shook his head from side to side and tried to hide his mounting fear. From behind where he now sat, Isaac heard Tiny ask what Scar meant by the accusation. Scar did not answer him directly, saying only that Isaac was "clever." Tiny looked flustered. He did not follow Scar's logic. But Isaac did, and knew he was in trouble. Grace seemed to as well because she asked Scar to leave them all alone. When he did not answer her, she repeated herself, even suggesting that Scar and Tiny had their money and bag of supplies so they should simply leave.

As soon as Isaac spoke, he realized he should have kept quiet. He asked, "She's right. Who are we going to tell?"

The look Scar gave Isaac made him shiver. As a cruel smile spread across his face, Scar answered the question: "No one. You're gonna tell no one."

He then reached down and jerked Isaac to his feet. Isaac

nearly fell again, then tried to break the grip of Scar's two hands. He could not. Scar dropped the bag of money he had been carrying and held Isaac in a vice-like grip on both his upper arms. Isaac felt himself being yanked harshly toward the rim of the crater. He dug his heels in and fought back, but Scar was too strong and shoved Isaac against the railing that marked the drop-off point of the crater. The caldera was rimmed by a protective rail fence that stood about four feet in height. Isaac could feel the intense heat coming from the lava below. Puffs of sulfur-laden smoke curled upward from the gaping, molten hole behind him.

Isaac heard Grace and Rebecca screaming "Stop it! What're you doing to him?" He could not see it, but Tiny was grabbing both girls and holding them tight against his enormous stomach to keep them from rushing to Isaac's side. Isaac was fighting for his life now, clawing back frantically, but Scar lifted him up to the top of the rail. As Scar was about to throw Isaac over the railing, he yelled out that he "was tired of these pesky kids!"

Flailing his arms in desperation, Isaac managed to hit Scar rather hardly on the ear and the violent little man momentarily let go of Isaac. But, Isaac could not find his footing on the rail and began to fall backward into the crater.

As his head fell backward, Isaac felt his feet fly up into the air, inadvertently kicking Scar in the chest. The fall seemed to happen in slow motion and Isaac felt a great panic overtake him as he realized he was falling backward into the molten hot crater. He opened his mouth to scream but nothing came out and then he landed awkwardly on the back of his head. There was a small lip of rock behind the protective railing that stretched a few feet toward the drop-off point. That is where Isaac landed. With a thud. He felt the pain shoot through the back of his head and his shoulder, but he knew he had not gone over the edge. In a quick flipping motion, Isaac hurled himself over onto his stomach and tried to raise his body to all fours. But out of the corner of his eye, he saw Scar lean through the opening between the middle two bars of the railing. Before he could move, Isaac saw Scar's boot speed toward him and connect with Isaac's ribs. The blow lifted Isaac off the ground and he felt his body fly off the rocky lip and down into the crater.

~~~

"Grandpa! You didn't say this would happen! Isaac can't fall into the volcano. He can't!" Andrew was in full protest over the realization of what his grandfather had just read from the old notebook.

"I know, Andy. I know. It was a horrible surprise."

Andrew remained upset as he spoke: "But what about Malama or Madam Pele? Didn't she tell Isaac in her dream to bring Scar and Tiny to her? Wasn't she going to take care of those criminals for the kids?"

"Isaac had that exact thought, and at that exact moment as

he fell into the caldera, Andy." Andrew's grandfather quickly returned to the old book in his lap.

~~~

Isaac did not have time to feel foolish for believing in his dream of Malama. He was off balance and falling into the caldera. But he felt a sharp pain under his left arm. A long pole stuck straight out from the inside wall of the caldera. It was only about two feet from the top of the rim. It caught Isaac under his arm and he grabbed a hold of it with a purpose, clenching it with both hands. As he caught the pole, his legs swung wildly to the side and nearly caused him to lose his grip. But he held on for dear life. From below his dangling feet Isaac could feel the heat of the lava. It felt as if the soles of his hiking shoes were beginning to melt and he thought his hair on the back of his head would suddenly catch fire. A burning sensation tinged the back of his legs and back of his neck.

From over the ledge above him, Isaac could hear the two girls screaming and Scar cursing at both them and Tiny. But Isaac could not make out any of the words. He concentrated on holding on and hoped that Scar would not throw Rebecca and Grace over the rim. The thought of his sister being carried to the railing forced Isaac to try and start climbing up the short distance to the ledge above. But, just as he pulled himself halfway up around the pole he saw Scar's head appear directly above him. It was so close he could smell Scar's foul breath. Both Scar and Isaac were startled at the sight of each other.

Isaac saw Scar adjusting his body, kneeling and leaning forward over the edge of the rim. His right hand came over the ledge, flailing downward at Isaac. Scar was screaming at Isaac as he swung wildly trying to knock Isaac off the pole but, once again, Isaac did not hear a word of it. He knew he was about to be pried free from the pole and forced down into the deep pool of lava. But then he had an idea.

Isaac tightened the grip with his left hand and let go of the pole with his right hand. He felt his body sway and could see Scar's hand trying to grab at his hair. But, in an instant, Isaac grabbed the pocket knife in his back right pocket – the one he hid earlier from Scar when his backpack was emptied out onto the ground. His thumb found the small knob that triggered a spring, which popped the three-inch blade out of the handle. Isaac felt the snap of the knife. As Scar grabbed a handful of Isaac's hair and began pulling him off the pole, Isaac swung the knife overhead with every ounce of strength he had. The knife hit its mark. The blade impaled itself into the middle of Scar's wrist. Isaac heard Scar shriek in pain. Isaac let go of the knife and grabbed the pole with both hands.

The blow forced Scar to release his grip on Isaac's hair. The red knife stuck at an odd angle out of Scar's wrist while his body lurched forward, off balance. Isaac could feel the hairy forearm, then the weight of Scar's shoulder hitting him as his full weight nearly fell on top of him. Isaac clung to the railing as Scar's body somersaulted overtop of Isaac.

Reflexively, Isaac turned and looked over his shoulder at Scar falling past him. Scar was screaming but still looking directly at Isaac and, for an instant, Isaac believed Scar would find a way of flying back up the lava wall and to the pole beside him. But as he watched, Isaac saw a bubbling fountain of lava explode up from the pool below. In the spray of bursting lava, Isaac saw the face of Malamalama – or Madam Pele. It appeared as molten fire. Her hair extended upward in flames of lava and seemed to grab Scar and envelope him, pulling him down into the fiery pit below.

That quickly there was no sign of Scar anywhere. He vanished into the lava, perhaps a hundred feet below from where Isaac's feet now dangled.

Isaac blinked tightly, trying to get the salty sweat out of his eyes. Looking up at the ledge of the crater just above his hands, Isaac managed a victorious smile and thought to himself: "Yeah, who's da man *now*, Bro."

Chapter 18

Lava

Tiny had watched in horror as Scar's body fell off the ledge of the crater. When this happened he inadvertently released his grip on both Rebecca and Grace. That is why the first thing Isaac saw above him were the faces of his two companions. They ran to the edge of the crater and peered over to look for Isaac. To their shock and delight, he was dangling from the pole which jutted straight out from the rocky wall of the crater.

As Isaac looked up at them, they both burst into tears of happiness. Isaac probably would have cried too, but he still had to climb out of the crater. As he told the girls to back up behind the railing, he pulled himself up on top of the pole, straddling it awkwardly. Once he had his balance, Isaac let go and grabbed the ledge of the crater just a short distance above him. One hand, then the other. Carefully. Pushing with his legs on the pole and pulling with his arms, Isaac climbed out of the crater. Grace immediately grabbed him, half hugging him and half pulling him over to the railing.

Both girls told Isaac they thought he was gone. They thought he had fallen into the lava. Isaac told them he had felt the same way! He did not bother, however, to tell them how it came to be that Scar fell off the ledge of the crater. That could wait. Directly in front of them was Tiny.

Tiny's face looked blank, as if he was still trying to process what had happened. Without taking his eyes off the big man, Isaac took the hands of his sister and friend and walked them slowly away from the crater. He wanted to put as much room as possible between himself and the molten lava.

After walking several feet away, not far enough away to worry Tiny that they might be running away – the thought of making a run for it had certainly crossed Isaac's mind, until he reasoned that Rebecca could not run. Her wrist still ached with every step and she was utterly exhausted and seemed to be losing energy by the hour. "No," Isaac thought to himself, "with Scar out of the picture, he might be able to negotiate with Tiny." As he was thinking that thought, Isaac saw something that would definitely improve his chance of negotiating with Tiny.

It was the bag of money Scar had carried, the money they had stolen from the Visitor Center of the park. It was only a few feet away from Isaac, and he sprinted to the bag before anyone responded or said a word. As Isaac slowly moved back beside the girls, money bag in hand, Tiny finally spoke.

"What happened?"

Isaac did not know what to say, so he said nothing.

Tiny repeated himself, "You tell me what happened."

In a calm voice Isaac said that Scar had fallen.

"But I hear da Boss scream." Tiny's mood darkened and he became visibly frustrated. "Dis crater is no good. I always know'd it was no good. It's Madam Pele. I tried ta tell Scar…"

Then Isaac tried something. He explained, "It was Madam Pele. You were right. I saw her come up and take Scar. She came out of the fire."

Tiny's eyes widened and his mouth dropped open. "See, I know dis crater is no good. Madam Pele is no good."

While he talked, Isaac was trying to figure a way out. He thought about trying to lure Tiny to the edge of the crater, but then realized that would not work. Tiny was so big that there was no way anyone was going to push him into the lava. He continued to brainstorm for ideas as he spoke.

"Now look, Tiny. We don't want any trouble. Never have. You and Scar had this money," Isaac held the bag in front of him as he spoke. "And you can still have it. We don't want it. But, just let us go."

Tiny interrupted Isaac by asking what he should do. Isaac responded by telling him to take the money and run, but to leave the kids alone. And then Isaac saw his way out. They were standing within the tourist viewing area but not far away was a sign that read "Danger – New Lava – Stay on the Trail." The sign was only about fifty yards away from the crater and tourist area, directly out into a black lava field marked with a temporary looking fence and signs. Nearby there were signs in other languages. Isaac recognized the word "cuidado" from school. He had taken Spanish classes in lower school.

Isaac also remembered that when fresh lava flowed, the hard crust of lava on the surface was very thin, much like ice on a frozen pond. The ancient lava where they now stood was several feet thick and had hardened hundreds or thousands of years before, and no lava flowed beneath the black surface. However, a fresh vent still had lava running through it, sometimes only a few feet below the hardened crust on the surface.

If only the three of them could lure Tiny toward the thin crust and then make a run for it. While he continued speaking to Tiny, Isaac reached behind himself and took Rebecca's hand. He gradually encouraged the two girls in the direction of the thin lava. They had covered a painstakingly slow twenty feet when Tiny finally noticed what was happening. His voice became angry, asking them where they thought they were going and why they were leaving him alone.

As Tiny was speaking Rebecca took off running. She could take the suspense no longer and ran in a uneven, stumbling stride away from Tiny and the crater. Tiny started to yell and took off after her. Fortunately for the children, he was not much faster than Rebecca. Isaac had hollered "no" several times before realizing it was to no avail. So, he too started running to catch up with Rebecca and Grace, who immediately ran after Rebecca.

He could hear Tiny's breathing behind them. It sounded like a great animal of some sort, huffing and puffing with each heavy step. Isaac looked over his shoulder twice and realized that, if he and Grace stayed with Rebecca, they were not going to outrun Tiny. He had no choice. They could not split up because he would not leave Rebecca again. So, Isaac led Rebecca and Grace in the direction of the "Danger" signs. As he ran, he could not help but think that they could not let Tiny catch them. They had all been through far too much for things to end here and now.

Tiny was only a few feet behind the children as they passed the first of the "Danger" signs. As he ran, Isaac threw the bag of money as hard as he could, swinging the bag in a full arch, overhead, then underhand, and heaving it as far as he could. The bag swung forward. It flew high in an arc over the signs and fencing, landing about fifty feet away.

The kids continued running, but Isaac could hear Tiny yelling to them. He was asking Isaac why he had thrown the bag. Then Isaac heard the heavy breathing stop and, as he turned and looked behind him, he saw Tiny stop at the edge of the fencing. He was staring out at the bag and still talking. Money was littered all across the thin crust of lava.

~~~

"I know what you are going to ask, Andy," grinned his grandfather. Out of the corner of his eye, he had seen Andrew leaning forward about to speak. "You want to know why Isaac threw the money away."

"Nooo, Grandpa." Andrew was mildly irritated that his grandfather would have thought that he had not figured out Isaac's crafty move. "What I was going to say was that Isaac is really smart. And cool. If Tiny wants the money, he'll have to go out on that dangerous lava to get it."

"Uh-huh," smiled his grandfather. "You're right. You really have this thing figured out, don't ya?"

"Well," boasted Andrew, "that's what I woulda done."

~~~

"That's da Boss's money," Tiny complained. "Look whatcha done." He spoke without looking at Isaac and the children. Rather, he continued staring at the money. Isaac, Grace, and Rebecca stopped running, but kept walking away from Tiny. They could no longer hear what he was saying but they watched him throw his leg over the railing and ungracefully heave his bulk to the other side.

Isaac felt like yelling to Tiny not to go out on the fresh lava flow, but he did not. At the site of Tiny tiptoeing gingerly across the thin crust of lava all three kids stopped walking. Without realizing it, Isaac was holding his breath. Tiny stretched his toes out in front of him very slowly, step by careful step. Nothing happened. Isaac knew he should get going and not let the girls watch what might happen, but he was transfixed and could not help but watch Tiny struggling across the thin crust.

As Isaac watched, he felt Rebecca's hand reach out and grab his own, then squeeze tightly. Tiny continued sliding slowly across the lava, tapping his toes then stepping as lightly as possible for a man of his enormous size. Five minutes had passed, then ten. Still, Tiny was only half way to the money bag.

And then it happened. As he tapped the crust in front of him, the ground under his back foot gave way. Tiny lurched backward, one arm circling over his head. His foot seemed to melt down into the lava for a moment and then he fell sideways in a heavy crash. Isaac heard Rebecca gasp, then realized that he too had gasped at the site.

Tiny did not move for a few minutes. Then he turned over on his stomach, raised his body to all fours, and began crawling across the lava. Two minutes later he reached the bag of money. But when he did, he did not move. Tiny remained motionless like a frozen statue on all fours. The children could not have known what Tiny had seen that froze him in this spot. What he saw was a hole in the black crust that revealed orange-red lava flowing only a few feet below the surface. Tiny stared at the hole, not daring to move.

As Isaac began telling the girls to start walking again, Tiny tried to stand. As he did, his foot again broke through the lava and he fell hard on his stomach. The bag of money landed nearby but just out of arm's reach. Isaac and the girls again stopped and watched. The bag landed half on and half in the hole in the crust. Very slowly, like a slinky walking down stairs, the contents within the bag shifted toward the hole and the bag slid below the crust and into the red lava. Two more times Tiny tried to stand, but the thin crust buckled beneath him. Finally, exhausted, frightened, and defeated, Tiny simply laid down on his stomach, not five feet from the bag of money had been. He did not move.

The kids did not speak. Isaac merely motioned with his head and the three of them turned and started walking up the hill in the direction of the Visitor Center. No one looked back. Tiny would not have noticed, as he was still sprawled out on the ground, face down.

Chapter 19

Rescue

Isaac led Rebecca and Grace along the small, paved road that ascended from the Halema'uma'u Crater up toward the Visitor Center. He did not know how far the Visitor Center was from the Crater, but that was where they were headed. The three children walked for about one hour before Rebecca needed to rest. When they sat down on the side of the road, it became immediately apparent to Isaac and Grace that Rebecca could go no farther. Her face was pale but her nose was badly sunburned, and the swelling in her wrist had not gone down. And they were out of water.

Fortunately, the elusive fern forest Isaac had mentioned to Scar turned out to be true and the children were able to get out of the direct sunlight. While Grace sat with Rebecca in the shade under a great fern leaf, Isaac walked up and down the road looking for coconut trees. They badly needed something to drink and eat. There were, however, none in sight anywhere. He thought momentarily of going back to where they had been, but realized that he had not seen a coconut tree since the day prior back by the ocean. Moreover, Isaac had decided that he would not leave Rebecca again.

Not knowing what to do, Isaac sat down beside the two girls. When he finally leaned back under a fern tree, he felt the weight and emotion of recent events. Sitting in the shade, finally free from Scar and Tiny, Isaac was overcome with joy and exhaustion at the same time. As he spoke to Grace, the two of them began to giggle deliriously. They felt "punch drunk" knowing they had cheated death several times.

"Well," smiled Isaac, "I believe we should ask for a refund when we get back to the hotel."

Grace laughed so hard, tears welled up in the sides of her eyes.

Then Isaac recounted the past two days. "I have had a lava tube collapse on me; was nearly squashed like a bug by falling rocks; fell and cut my leg on sharp lava rocks; and then was tossed about in a tsunami… let's see, what else? Oh yea, broke my nose; skinned my knee trying to cross a huge hole in the earth – and it still really hurts; I was kidnapped by two criminals; punched by one of them; fell out of a tall coconut tree and I nearly died in a fiery crater…"

"Don't forget," reminded Grace, "we've lived on nothing but coconuts and a granola bar!"

"Oh yea, and that too. And the granola bar was the worst of it!" Isaac laughed.

Sitting there thinking of the list of predicaments, scrapes, and adventures they had been through made Isaac's nose, knee, and back ache all the more. And then Isaac realized what he had not mentioned: that Spike was gone and they could not find their parents. He quietly whispered these thoughts to Grace, who added that Keiko and her parents were also still missing. Both children sat in silence for a few moments then admitted that they missed Isaac's parents, Keiko, and even Spike. Both felt the tears coming, so they stopped talking. Isaac said a quiet prayer to Malamalama, asking her to help him find the others.

Isaac wanted to get up and continue toward the Visitor Center, but he knew Rebecca was in no shape to travel. Looking over at Grace, he realized that she was in no shape to walk either. Her one shoe had completely worn out. Half her foot was exposed and was riddled with red welts and blisters. He looked up at Grace and saw her looking at him. She had seen him staring at her sore foot, a concerned look on his face.

"Don't worry," she grinned. "I'm tough."

She denied that it hurt much, but Isaac knew better. Then, as Grace asked him how he was feeling, Isaac had to admit that he too was also in no condition to travel. That made three of them.

"We're a sight for sore eyes, Grace."

Grace agreed. Isaac was thinking of a way to ask Grace

what she thought they should do about Rebecca and getting her water when he heard a familiar sound.

~~~

"What sound, Grandpa? Not another tsunami!"

"No, fortunately it wasn't another tsunami," his grandfather assured him.

"That's good because I don't think I could take it any more. Goodness, Grandpa, I don't think Isaac could either. How could Isaac have done all that?"

"Well, Tiger, I don't think Isaac could have taken anything else either. But, this time it was good news." And the old man smiled as he turned the next page.

~~~

It was the sound of a helicopter approaching. Isaac recognized it immediately and struggled to stand up. Every bone in his body hurt but he mustered the strength to stand. He stripped off his torn, dirty shirt and began waving it over his head like a crazed person. Even if the people in the helicopter could not possibly hear him, Isaac nonetheless started to yell and scream.

Grace joined in, and even Rebecca perked up enough to mutter a weak "help." Grace and Isaac ran up and down the road waving their hands, as Isaac thought to himself that this time they might finally catch a break. The helicopter could not miss them again!

And it did not. As the great, blue bird flew overhead, Isaac noticed that it descended quite a bit then turned around for another pass by them. It was getting lower and lower. Though the sun hurt his eyes as he looked upward, Isaac thought he saw people in the helicopter waving back at them.

The pilot set the blue helicopter down in the middle of the road. Isaac and Grace backed up as it approached and felt the strong blast of wind from the rotating blades above the main body of the helicopter. Isaac covered his eyes as dust blew ferociously in his direction, but he heard the sound of the helicopter shutting down. The winding blades grew gradually slower and quieter. As it did, Isaac and Grace ran to Rebecca's side and helped her up to her feet.

When the door of the fuselage opened, Isaac thought he would burst with happiness and relief. His mother, followed by his father, bounded out of the craft and ran toward him, ducking as everyone does when they are near a helicopter. The three children met them halfway and it was the most emotional reunion Isaac had ever experienced. Hugs. Tears. More hugs and tears. They all laughed with joy! As his parents bubbled on and on about how much they missed the children and how much they loved them, it was Isaac who finally raised his voice.

"We need to get Rebecca to a hospital. Her wrist is broken." As he yelled over the sound of the helicopter engine, the park ranger who had flown in the passenger seat appeared behind his parents. He was holding a large container that turned out to be a first aid kit. Before opening it, however, he handed Grace a large thermos of water. Grace, then Rebecca, then Isaac took turns gulping the water. It flowed down everyone's faces and throats, and they succeeded in drinking the entire half gallon in minutes despite the ranger's repeated requests to slow down. A second thermos was fetched from the chopper and Isaac poured it over his head. It was the best "bath" of his life!

It was then that Isaac's mother asked about Spike. When all three children grew quiet, the worry lines across Mrs. Sanders' forehead became more pronounced. No one answered. Isaac only lowered his eyes and shook his head in the negative. His parents understood.

The pilot flew the chopper to the Hilo Medical Center in the largest city nearest to the volcano. It was only a short flight and the feeling of being reunited with family made it go all the faster. Isaac did not elaborate on what had happened to Spike. Nor did he tell his parents about Scar or Tiny. There was ample time for all of that later, and he did not want to alarm his mother about the full extent of the ordeal they had survived.

As everyone exited the helicopter at the hospital, Isaac told his parents to go with Rebecca. After a brief explanation of who Keiko happened to be and how she happened to become separated from them, he informed them that he had to go back to find Keiko and her parents. Isaac told them he had made a promise and intended to keep it. Isaac's father reluctantly agreed but only on the condition that he accompany Isaac to find Keiko. He recognized a firmness in his son's resolve and decided to support it rather than try and talk him out of it.

Mrs. Sanders and Grace kept Rebecca company, as a uniformed nurse brought the little girl a wheel chair and made quite a fuss over her. After a quick exchange of hugs – and more tears from his mother – Isaac said a quick goodbye and ran back into the helicopter. The excitement over being rescued recharged his batteries and Isaac was now bound and determined to find Keiko.

"I know where she might be," he yelled to the pilot and park ranger, who were sitting in the front of the helicopter. Both men nodded from the front seats that they knew the spot Isaac mentioned. Isaac hoped Keiko would be there. The old town that had been covered with lava was a popular place for tourists taking helicopter tours. And off they went. As the helicopter banked toward the ocean and the volcano, Isaac also told the park ranger about Scar and Tiny, and the big prisoner's whereabouts near the Hale Ma'uma'u Crater. The ranger radioed the sheriff's office, who dispatched two police helicopters to the site.

While Isaac was saying his goodbyes to his mother, sister, and Grace, his father had hit the vending machine in the hospital lobby. As the helicopter raced low over the treetops, Isaac inhaled a donut-like Hawaiian pastry called a malasada and two bags of Maui Onion Chips. At that moment, they beat anything on the menu of the fancy restaurant at their resort.

As he gulped the food, Isaac told his father and the ranger the details of their encounter with Scar and Tiny. The ranger continued to transmit by radio to the sheriff's office the details of Isaac's description of Tiny and the details of Scar's demise. Over the crackling radio and sound of the blades beating the air, Isaac heard the police dispatcher discussing coordinates with the pilot and ranger. He also heard the skeptical tone in the police dispatcher's voice. Two police helicopters were on their way. But, Isaac knew they doubted the fantastical details of his story.

As Isaac continued relaying information on Keiko and her parents, his father turned ghostly pale at the thought of his son nearly being thrown into the crater by a convicted murderer. But, when Isaac finished the story his father gave him a crushing hug. All three of the men in the helicopter believed Isaac and agreed that he showed courage and resourcefulness. His father repeated the praise over and over until Isaac had to stop him: "Daaad, enough already."

Only fifteen minutes after flying into the airspace of the volcano to search for Keiko, the ranger spotted her. Using binoculars as they sped low over the remains of the ancient Hawaiian trail, the ranger noticed her bright shirt against the black lava. Keiko was weak and dehydrated, but alive. She managed a friendly smile and a few soft shrieks when she opened her eyes and saw Isaac bounding from the helicopter and across the lava field toward her.

Before heading to the hospital, however, Isaac asked the pilot to stop just uphill from the Thurston Lava Tube, the last location he had seen Keiko's parents. The pilot and ranger agreed but said that a sweep over the area with the helicopter was more efficient. As the chopper buzzed the tree line, Isaac, his father, and even Keiko peered out the windows looking for the Okinakas. After several unsuccessful sweeps, the pilot said that they had to get Keiko to the hospital. He promised, however, to return to look for the Okinakas. Isaac surprised himself as he confidently and boldly said "no!" The pilot had to drop him off on the ground to continue the search. Only then would Isaac agree that the chopper could take Keiko to the Hilo Medical Center. Isaac's father again reluctantly agreed. He had seen the way Keiko calmed down when she saw Isaac. He scarcely recognized this new take-charge attitude from his son and informed the pilot rather forcefully that his son had been through enough. They had to honor his request. Keiko, in passable English spoken in a weak voice, told the men that Isaac had saved everyone.

The pilot agreed and landed. With a quick hug, Isaac promised Keiko they'd find her parents. Then, Isaac, his father, and the park ranger jumped out of the open door and watched the chopper lift slowly into the air, circle once, and speed off in the direction of Hilo.

"I hope you know, young man, that your mother is going to kill me," Isaac's father commented. "When she sees that helicopter land without you in it…"

"She'll get over it," smiled Isaac.

The ranger asked Isaac to point them in the last known direction of the Okinakas, which he did, and the three of them set off.

As the helicopter sped off toward the Hilo Medical Center for the second time that day, the park ranger, whose name was Aleki, pointed out the way to the Visitor Center. Ranger Aleki carried a small backpack with water and a first aid kit, and he assured Isaac that everything would be fine. Isaac agreed. The ranger even mentioned that they were prepared in the event Tiny had managed to escape the thin lava crust of the crater. As they spoke, Aleki said two helicopters full of deputies were nearby and he also patted the pistol on his hip. Seeing the gesture sent a shiver rushing down Isaac's spine. It was the same motion used by Scar. Of course, the ranger could not have known what Scar had done. At the thought of Scar, Isaac involuntarily turned and looked around. Isaac knew that Scar was gone, but he could not help but feel a bit vulnerable walking through the fern forest.

Only a few hundred feet up the road, they found Yoshi and Masume Okinaka. The couple was sitting on a bed of ferns and had to be stirred from their sleep by Isaac. The Okinakas were extremely dehydrated and weak. Yoshi had a very high fever and looked in bad shape. But when Isaac informed them that Keiko was being choppered to the hospital at that very moment, both parents perked up. The ranger radioed the police helicopters and the chopper carrying Keiko, which had just landed at the hospital, to inform them that they had found the Okinakas. Aleki gave the coordinates of his location, and the police helicopters radioed that they were only minutes away.

Before Yoshi and Masume accepted water, however, they insisted on speaking to Keiko by radio. It was a cheerful moment as everyone – including Isaac and Ranger Aleki – smiled. Isaac could not understand Keiko's words because she spoke in Japanese to her parents, and he doubted they could make them out even if he did speak Japanese because of the heavy crackle of the radio. But it did not matter.

Moments later, a police helicopter landed on the road near them. Two burly sheriff's deputies emerged from the first helicopter and began asking Isaac questions about Scar and Tiny. As Isaac talked, a small party gathered around him. Everyone except Isaac's father and Aleki found it very hard to believe his story, as they were familiar with Scar's reputation and Tiny's bulk.

The officer in charge, hands on his hips, bellowed, "Come on! You expect us to believe that a kid survived an earthquake, tsunami, and an encounter with those two criminals. Never. Scar DiSilva was one of the worst we ever had on this island, son!"

John Sanders interrupted the uniformed officers. "Hey,"

he yelled, "if my son says this happened, it happened!"

When Masume Okinaka heard Mr. Sanders identify himself as Isaac's father, she walked briskly to the circle of men around Isaac and injected herself into the conversation. In broken English she too scolded the police officer. "My daughter said that this man's son saved all three of the girls. And if it were not for him, my husband and I would not be alive today."

Masume then turned and spoke in rapid and firm words to her husband, who was being lifted onto a stretcher by two more sheriff's deputies. Yoshi immediately pushed aside the deputies who were helping him, and barked a string of angry words at the other two officers.

Masume translated, "I would tell you what he said," she screamed at the men, "but I think you already know. My husband said that this boy saved all of us. And that he is a hero!"

The deputies apologized. The senior officer grabbed Isaac's hand and asked him if he would please accept his sincere apology. Isaac simply nodded his head and told them that they had to get the Okinakas to the hospital.

As Mr. and Mrs. Okinaka were helped onto the helicopter, a paramedic from the second police chopper tended to the Okinakas' injuries. All the while, Isaac could hear Yoshi Okinaka protesting bitterly in Japanese. Isaac did not speak the language, but knew Mr. Okinaka was complaining that the doctor should treat his wife first.

"And you, too, young man," said the paramedic, motioning for Isaac to join the Okinakas.

But Isaac declined.

~~~

Isaac's father motioned for his son to climb aboard the helicopter and turned to offer Isaac his hand. But, once again, Isaac said he had one more thing to attend to and could not yet leave the volcano.

John Sanders shook his head, smiling, and laughed. "Of course not, you need to rescue the whole island!"

There was no way the men, including the police and his father, were going to force Isaac onto the helicopter heading back to the hospital. As the helicopter carrying the Okinakas and the paramedic lifted off, John Sanders turned to the assembled group of deputies and said that it looked as if Isaac was still in charge! They all smiled. It was clear from the corroborating stories of the Okinakas and Keiko, as well as from Grace and Rebecca, that all of what Isaac said was true. The burly police officer who initially questioned Isaac, even straightened his back and saluted him, saying "Alright, Captain, what is our next move?"

And so, Isaac, his father, and Ranger Aleki joined the deputies on the first of the two police helicopters.

"What now?" John Sanders was yelling over the roar of the engine and spinning prop above them. "Where are we going?"

"To the Hale Ma'uma'u Crater. There's one more thing I've gotta do, Dad!"

Ordinarily, Isaac's father would have asked a hundred questions and demanded an answer, but Isaac's tone and confidence were such that he just sat back for the ride, although he did throw one arm around Isaac's shoulders as they flew.

No sooner had they lifted off than the pilot turned and motioned with his hand that they should all look to their left. As Isaac and his father leaned over Ranger Aleki for a look, they heard the one deputy announce "Roger. That's him, alright. The big one. I can tell from up here." And below them Isaac could see the orange jump suit worn by Tiny. He was still sprawled facedown on the thin crust of fresh lava near the crater.

"Now, how're we gonna get him?" The deputy in the front seat turned and spoke to his colleague sitting in the back seats beside Isaac, directly across from Isaac and looking out the door.

"Don't know. Maybe we'd better call a tow truck!"

The deputies burst out in laughter. Isaac could not have known but there was a major manhunt on the island. Every law enforcement official in the state was sent to the Big Island to deal with the crisis of the earthquake and tsunamis, but some members of the sheriff's department were assigned to the task of finding the two escaped convicts.

"You're lucky, Son," said the officer in front of Isaac. Without taking his eyes off Tiny below, he continued speaking.

"Those two guys – Scar DiSilva and his partner, Tiny Salavea, the big Samoan – are, er ah, make that *were* bad news. You don't even want to know what's on their rap sheet! They're about the worst we've ever come across."

Isaac looked at his father with a curious expression. Mr. Sanders explained that a "rap sheet" was a list of all the crimes they had committed.

"Yes, sir, Son. You must be one tough compadre or one lucky kid to still be alive. That Scar DiSilva..." But the officer decided he should not finish what he was going to say. Finally, the deputy looked up and smiled at Isaac while shaking his head from side to side in disbelief. For a third time that day, Isaac's father beamed with pride as the deputy said what an impressive young man John Sanders had raised.

"Look!" It was the pilot. As he was maneuvering the helicopter to the parking lot next to the crater and spot where Tiny was located he saw something. "I can't believe it. He moved. That big Samoan's still alive!"

Mr. Sanders was shocked to see his son smile and pump his fist into the air. He could swear Isaac seemed happy at the news. While hovering several feet above the thin crust of the lava, the other helicopter began lowering a rescue device from a steel winch outside the door.

Chapter 20

?

Answers

The children were finally back at their hotel. Rebecca sported a pink cast over her wrist with signatures from the hospital staff as well as several police officers, a park ranger, the pilot of the helicopter that had flown her to the medical center, and even reporters who flocked to the hospital for the amazing story. When Rebecca was released, the entire family enjoyed a helicopter ride across the island to their resort and, when they entered the front doors, several of the hotel staff greeted them with a great cheer. Two Hawaiian men played ukuleles and sang, while an attractive young woman offered each member of the Sanders party a flower lei. Isaac smiled and whispered to Grace that it seemed like a lifetime ago when they had all received flowers at the airport! The manager then introduced herself and presented Rebecca and Grace with beautiful bouquets of tropical flowers, and

Isaac with an envelope. It was a very fancy envelope and as large as a clipboard.

Everyone seemed to lean in next to Isaac to see the contents of the envelope as he opened it. Isaac chuckled at the scene, as it reminded him of the children from the movie about Willie Wonka's chocolate factory opening the Wonka bars looking for the golden ticket. In fact, the "ticket" turned out to be golden, both in color and in content. It was a voucher redeemable for a free week vacation at the resort for the whole family. Isaac ignored the applause, thanked everyone, and made eye contact with his parents. His meaning was clear to them: he simply wanted to go to the room and sleep. He was also thinking of Spike and he had some unanswered questions for Kalani and Malamalama from the luau. Isaac was sound asleep within seconds of taking a shower. He missed the grand buffet that his parents had ordered from room service. Grace and Rebecca ate until their stomachs hurt but there was still plenty remaining for Isaac when he woke up.

Isaac awoke the next day after sleeping for over twelve hours. His sister and Grace were still asleep. It was the smell of food that stirred him from his deep slumber. And an empty stomach. Mrs. Sanders had ordered a spread of food fit for an army. And it was a good thing because Isaac ate his fill – three times over. He never thought something could taste so good. Once Grace and Rebecca were awake, Isaac excused himself, telling his parents he needed to go to the main desk in order to ask the manager a question. Mr. and Mrs. Sanders immediately said they would join him, but Isaac told them he had to talk to two of the hotel employees by himself.

Both his parents and Grace asked him what he needed to do, but Isaac only told them it was personal and important.

~~~

"What could it be? Isaac isn't going to go anywhere, is he, Grandpa? Like back to the volcano?"

Andrew's grandfather did not respond. He simply chuckled and shook his head "no." The old man slowly took off his glasses and closed the frayed notebook. He finished the story from memory.

~~~

In the main lobby, Isaac asked a friendly clerk if he could speak to the manager. The clerk recognized Isaac as their resident hero – the kid who survived the earthquake, tsunami, and a bout with two criminals. She had seen the coverage on the local television channel. The clerk was especially friendly and went to get the manager. Overhearing the conversation, a bellhop standing by the door – a twenty-year-old Hawaiian boy who looked like he had just stepped out of a surfer magazine – walked over to Isaac. He handed Isaac a bowl full of tasty macadamia nuts and winked, telling Isaac to try the chocolate-covered ones.

The manager – the same lady who had given him the gold gift certificate the day prior, a petite woman whose nametag listed "Ellen Kusano" – smiled a warm "aloha" as she shook Isaac's hand. However, she instantly noticed Isaac's serious demeanor. He asked her if he could talk to the two main performers from the resort's luau. Isaac informed Ms. Kusano that he and his family had attended a luau the night before they went to the volcano and he had met the hostess, an old woman named Malamalama, and a large Hawaiian man named Kalani.

Isaac was stunned at what the manager told him. Ms. Kusano said that they did not have anyone with those names working at the luau. When Isaac described both Malama and Kalani in great detail, the manager maintained her point. Shaking her head in deep thought, she told Isaac that it was an attractive, young woman who was the host for the luau show, but that her name was Leilani. She also told him that there were about eight female cast members, but that all of them were dancers, and all of them were young. She described a man named Kaipo who blew the conch but said he was the same thin fellow who climbed the coconut tree with the machete.

Isaac insisted that she must be mistaken, so Ms. Kusano called her assistant manager, who appeared a few minutes later. He repeated everything Isaac was already told and the clerk who had helped Isaac nodded in agreement, saying she knew most of the cast members and had never even seen the two individuals Isaac described. As Isaac mumbled that he did not understand how this was possible, the bellhop who helped guests with their luggage – the boy who looked like a surfer – spoke up. He informed his manager that he had an idea.

The surfer walked beside Isaac as he led him out of the resort lobby and to the area where the luau show takes place. There were locker rooms for the employees nearby and the surfer told Isaac he would introduce him to one of the cast members who came early to prepare the pig for the evening feast. This man had been working at the luau longer than anyone at the hotel.

Isaac was sure that everyone in the lobby was mistaken and that the cast member would tell him what he wanted to hear. The surfer and Isaac found the old man near the cooking pit, cleaning the area in advance of the evening show. But, again to Isaac's dismay, the man told him that he had never met anyone matching the description. Plus, the cook said, he had worked with the luau longer than any of the other dancers, singers, or musicians. He knew everyone in the show.

As the surfer led a dejected Isaac back to his hotel room, he asked the boy why he was so set on meeting the people he called Malamalama and Kalani. At first, Isaac dismissed the question, saying that the surfer would not understand. But, after the surfer continued to press the question, Isaac stopped and looked his new pal in the eyes.

Isaac started his explanation by saying that the story he

was about to tell would sound "weird" and "impossible." Isaac described how he had met Kalani and Malama at the luau and how they both spoke to him, and seemed to take a very special interest in him. He then shared with his surfer friend how the two of them visited him in his dreams and...

That was when the surfer interrupted Isaac. The twinkle in his eyes and his light demeanor changed. He grew serious as he finished Isaac's sentence, telling him that the two characters probably gave Isaac advice that helped him during the earthquake and tsunami. Isaac's mouth dropped and he only nodded his head in agreement. The surfer continued, telling Isaac that when he first heard the boy's description of the old lady he knew that is must be her. The surfer described both Malama and Kalani in perfect detail.

"Who? Malama?" Isaac demanded.

"Who do ya think?" the surfer answered. "Madam Pele herself."

Isaac gasped. He knew it sounded unbelievable and yet, as soon as he heard the name, he knew exactly that it was her. Everything came into focus for him and he understood the full nature of his dreams. Madam Pele had comforted him throughout the ordeal at the volcano.

"Of course," Isaac agreed. "Madam Pele lives in the crater – Hale Ma'uma'u. But, then, who was..."

"Kalani," both boys said the name in unison.

"Yea, right. If Kalani was as big as you say. Tattoos right? Strong arms? Funny? And..." continued the surfer.

Isaac cut him off, agreeing loudly with each description. Then the surfer said, "Right. Kalani is Kamehameha." The wink and smile returned.

"You mean the great Hawaiian king?" Isaac knew the answer but asked the question anyway.

"None other, dude."

Isaac was so relieved to hear what the surfer had just told him that he jumped out and hugged his friend. "Easy, dude," was the response. The surfer told Isaac that many of the older Hawaiians believed that Madam Pele and King Kamehameha appeared in human form. He went on, explaining how his grandmother always told him stories of how Pele and Kamehameha's spirits still haunted the island and helped those in need, especially young Hawaiian children and people who showed great "aloha" and respect for the "aina," meaning the Hawaiian land.

And with that explanation, the surfer gave Isaac a "shaka" sign with his hand, winked, and took off his necklace. It was a stone petroglyph – a carving made from ancient volcanic rock featuring a hook that looked to Isaac like either a fishing hook or a weapon. The surfer then became serious. He offered Isaac his "aloha" for respecting the "aina" and then turned to head back to the lobby.

Isaac ran to his room to tell his family but, as his hand turned the doorknob, he decided against it. No one else had remembered seeing Malama and Kalani, and neither Rebecca nor Grace had dreamed about Madam Pele or Kamehameha.

No, Isaac decided that story would be one he kept to himself.

~~~

"No way, Grandpa! That is awesome!"

"Yes, Andy, and that is how it stayed. Isaac never did tell his parents or even his sister." Andrew's grandfather stood up slowly from his rocking chair beside the bed, stretched his sore back, and then sat down on the edge of the bed beside his grandson.

His grandfather continued, "The only one he ever told was Grace. You see, Andy, I've kept that story to myself all these years. Didn't even tell your parents." Andrew interrupted his grandfather with a stammering sound, as if he were trying to spit out a complicated word. But then his eyes lit up and he jumped out of the bed and on top of his grandfather, nearly knocking him off the bed.

"No way, Grandpa! You were Isaac? I mean, you *are* Isaac? But, how… Unbelievable!"

Then Andrew made a shaka sign with his hand and told his Grandfather Isaac that he was "the most awesome Bruddah!"

And so Andrew's grandfather told the end to the story. He said he "lived happy ever after." He ended up marrying Grace when they were in their twenties and had two daughters, one of whom was Andrew's mother. Although

Malama and Kalani had never again visited Grandpa Isaac in his dreams, he thought often of them, and of his extraordinary adventure on the Big Island of Hawaii so many years ago. It was just within the past few years – since he had become a grandfather – that he started to think about going back to Hawaii, a place he had not visited since that memorable vacation during his childhood. Andrew could not believe his grandfather had not been back to Hawaii since the incident.

These thoughts had prompted Grandpa Isaac to dig out the old notebook that had been locked away ever since he finished writing it as a teenager. It was the same frayed book that now sat on his lap.

"Yes, Andy, I've been thinking that it's about time to go back..."

"And perhaps take your grandson with you!" Andrew finished his grandfather's sentence with an eager look in his eyes. Grandpa Isaac nodded in agreement and they both smiled.

And as the two of them embraced in a warm hug, the old book fell onto the floor. The faded gold certificate for a free Hawaiian vacation fell open beside it.

About the Authors

Alex Watson is a middle school student who was born in Hawaii but now resides in Boca Raton, Florida, where he enjoys hiking, playing music, and spending days at the beach. He hiked across the Hawaiian volcanoes described in this book. Although this is his first book, he has plenty of ideas for more of them!

Robert P. Watson is a professor at Lynn University in Florida who has published many books on American politics and history. He is also Alex's father.

Alex and Robert encourage parents and children to read and write together. They welcome you to the "Let's Write Together" community, featuring writing tips, contests and awards for child-parent writing teams. Learn more at www.LetsWriteTogether.com.